Editor

Marisa Maccarelli-Harris, M.A.

Managing Editor

Mara Ellen Guckian

Editor in Chief

Karen J. Goldfluss, M.S. Ed.

Creative Director

Sarah M. Smith

Illustrator

Clint McKnight

Cover Artist

Barb Lorseyedi

Art Coordinator

Renée Mc Elwee

Imaging

James Edward Grace
Craig Gunnell

Publisher

Mary D. Smith, M.S. Ed.

Author

Sandra Cook, M.A.
Helen Leon, M.A.

For correlations to the Common Core State Standards, see pages 8–9.
Correlations can also be found at
http://www.teachercreated.com/standards.

Teacher Created Resources

6421 Industry Way
Westminster, CA 92683
www.teachercreated.com

ISBN: 978-1-4206-3946-9

© 2014 Teacher Created Resources
Made in U.S.A.

Table of Contents

Teacher Overview

Math Problem-solving Tests

Answer Key

Introduction

It is Wednesday afternoon and the teacher has just announced a math test for Friday. Across the classroom, hearts start to race. Looks of dread appear on the faces of the students. Taking a test can be very stressful. Can you remember a time when you studied very hard and thought you knew everything, but you received the test results and were shocked to see a grade that was much lower than you had expected? What happened? Well, you might have known the material, but there is more to taking a test than just knowing the material. To be successful when taking a test, you must also know test-taking strategies.

Taking tests is not something new, but the number of tests taken by a student and the importance of those tests is. This math problem-solving book focuses on the skills included in the Common Core State Standards that are prevalent on standardized, multiple-choice tests. This book concentrates on understanding the various types of math problems that may be presented for a particular skill and how to evaluate the problems in order to solve them. From preparing students to recognize tricky questions designed to confuse them, to exercises that emphasize the importance of discriminating necessary facts from unnecessary ones, this book gives students the tools and the experience to enable them to critically analyze and solve grade-level-appropriate math problems.

Students will learn test-taking skills needed to become more confident and efficient test takers. Furthermore, students will gain critical-thinking skills that can be used in many situations throughout their test-taking years and beyond.

How the Book Is Organized

This book is organized into three tests: Test A, Test B, and Test C. Each test has 100 questions that are aligned to the Common Core State Standards. Different types of questions are included to familiarize students with strategies that are crucial to successful test taking.

There are four questions on each page of the three tests. For continuity, the skill is the same for each question number across all three tests, which means question 14 tests the same skill on Test A as it does on Test B, and later on Test C. These assessments were designed so that the degree of call-out assistance provided decreases from Test A to Test B, with no call-outs on Test C.

Test A

Test A provides students with specific and detailed guidance regarding how to approach each math problem. Call-outs appear as rectangular-shaped boxes that are positioned beside the questions. These call-outs give the students specific information to help solve the problem.

Example from Test A

Directions: Read the word problem carefully. Select the best answer for each question.

Melissa has 3 dogs. She bought 21 dog treats for them. She wants to give each dog the same number of treats. How many treats will each dog get?

25. Which clue helps you decide which operation to use to solve the problem?

   A. has 3 dogs

   B. each

   C. how many

   D. bought dog treats

> The clue word in this problem means that you should divide.

26. Which equation shows the solution to the problem?

   A. 21 x 3 = 63

   B. 24 ÷ 3 = 8

   C. 21 – 3 = 18

   D. 21 ÷ 3 = 7

> Find the total number of dog treats and how many dogs Melissa has. Remember, Melissa wants to *share* the treats *equally* between her 3 dogs.

How the Book Is Organized *(cont.)*

Example from Test A *(cont.)*

Test A offers assistance to properly "decode" each question. Work with students throughout this test and encourage critical thinking. Try these suggestions:

- Have students underline important facts in order to draw attention to their importance in the solution of the problem.
- Highlight or circle word clues or phrases that tell which operation to use.
- Go over the test as a group, reviewing it line by line to help interpret each problem and each possible answer.

Consider the example from Test A. You might underline *3 dogs* and *21 dog treats* because they are number facts that are important to the problem's solution. You could circle *will each dog get* because it is a clue that using division solves the problem.

Test B

Test B continues to provide call-out support, but there are fewer call-outs. Students should continue to practice test-taking strategies on Test B, such as underlining important facts and highlighting or circling key words and phrases. It offers the teacher a chance to assess which math skills still need additional work.

Example from Test B

Directions: Read the word problem carefully. Select the best answer for each question.

There are 6 players on a hockey team. At the skating rink, 8 teams were playing. How many players were at the rink in all?

25. Which addition sentence is equal to 8 x 6?
   A. 8 + 8 + 8 + 8 + 8 + 8 + 8 + 8
   B. 8 + 6
   C. 6 + 6 + 6 + 6 + 6 + 6 + 6 + 6
   D. 8 − 6

26. What is the answer to the problem above?
   A. 8 x 6 = 48 teams
   B. 8 + 6 = 14 players
   C. 8 x 6 = 48 players
   D. 48 ÷ 6 = 8 players

> 8 x 6 means that there were 8 teams and that there were 6 people on each team.

How the Book Is Organized *(cont.)*

Test C

Test C also provides 100 questions, but no call-out support is provided. It is an opportunity for students to take a math problem-solving assessment independently. This test will give both you and your students an opportunity to see the degree to which they have internalized not only the ability to correctly identify skills needed to solve the problem, but the specific strategies they can employ to answer each question.

Answer Key

The answer key at the back of this book is designed to be another test-taking tool for both teachers and students. A student bubble sheet is also provided on page 112.

While it is important for students to know which answer is correct, it is equally useful for students to understand why other options are incorrect. The answer key provides explanations for the correct answers to the questions. Each incorrect answer is also discussed to provide students with possible explanations for why they might have chosen it.

The following excerpt from the answer key shows the answer to one of the questions in the example from Test B on the previous page.

Sample Answer Key Explanation

---

25. Correct Answer: C

$6 + 6 + 6 + 6 + 6 + 6 + 6 + 6 = 8 \times 6$. Adding 6 eight times means 6 players were on 8 teams: $6 + 6 + 6 + 6 + 6 + 6 + 6 + 6 = 48$. 6×8 means the 6 players on each team were multiplied by 8 teams, and it also equals 48.

Incorrect Answers:

A. $8 + 8 + 8 + 8 + 8 + 8 + 8 + 8 = 8 \times 8$. 8×8 means 8 players were multiplied by 8 teams. There were only 6 players on each team.

B. $8 + 6$ does not equal 8×6. $8 + 6 = 14$. It is the number of teams added to the number of players per team. It does not compute the total number of players on all the teams.

D. $8 - 6$ does not equal 8×6. $8 - 6$ is subtracting the number of players on each team from the number of teams. It does not indicate the total number of players on the 8 teams.

How to Use the Book

Teachers know that students learn differently. Each class tends to be strong in some skill areas and weak in others. Therefore, it is up to the teacher to decide how to use this book to best benefit the students. Consider the following possibilities:

The book can be completed in the order it has been written. Test A can be completed first, then Test B, and finally Test C. Teachers will lend less support in Test B than in Test A, and Test C can be administered as a true test to assess students' skills.

Or, the book can be completed in smaller increments, depending on the needs of the class. Since each test has 100 questions, consider dividing the tests into parts. For example, assign problems 1–20 on Test A. Carefully review the questions on this test, along with the call-outs, with the class. Assign the same 20 questions on Test B, and review the responses as a group. Finally, assign questions 1–20 on Test C. Test C does not contain any call-outs; students should complete it independently. After completing Test C independently, each question can be reviewed orally and modeled, if necessary, so the students can understand why each answer is correct or incorrect. Any observed weaknesses should be addressed as they arise. Another approach to Test C would be for the teacher to collect and grade the test after students independently complete it. Any areas of weakness should be reviewed and modeled as a class or in a small-group setting.

Why is **B** an incomplete answer to the question?

All answers should be reviewed so students know why an answer was incorrect. Make this an appealing activity by declaring the students to be detectives! When reviewing answers to the questions, have each student come up with a reason why someone would make that mistake. For example, the student might state that the problem was wrong because the number facts were added instead of subtracted. Finding the reason for the incorrect answer will help students understand the problem and solve the mystery.

In addition, the tests can be used as study tools. Place the tests and answer sheets in a binder that is accessible to students. They can "self-test" before and between assessments (including standardized tests) to maintain skills and focus on test-taking strategies.

Common Core State Standards Correlation

Each question in *Critical Thinking: Test-taking Practice for Math (Grade 3)* meets one or more of the following Common Core State Standards © Copyright 2010. National Governors Association Center for Best Practices and Council of Chief State School Officers. All rights reserved. For more information about these standards, go to *http://www.corestandards.org/* or *http://www.teachercreated.com/standards*.

Operations & Algebraic Thinking	Problem #s
Represent and solve problems involving multiplication and division.	
Math.3.OA.A.3 Use multiplication and division within 100 to solve word problems in situations involving equal groups, arrays, and measurement quantities, e.g., by using drawings and equations with a symbol for the unknown number to represent the problem.	13–16, 17–20, 25–28, 31-32
Understand properties of multiplication and the relationship between multiplication and division.	
Math.3.OA.B.5 Apply properties of operations as strategies to multiply and divide. *Examples: If 6 × 4 = 24 is known, then 4 × 6 = 24 is also known. (Commutative property of multiplication.) 3 × 5 × 2 can be found by 3 × 5 = 15, then 15 × 2 = 30, or by 5 × 2 = 10, then 3 × 10 = 30. (Associative property of multiplication.) Knowing that 8 × 5 = 40 and 8 × 2 = 16, one can find 8 × 7 as 8 × (5 + 2) = (8 × 5) + (8 × 2) = 40 + 16 = 56. (Distributive property.)*	21–24
Solve problems involving the four operations, and identify and explain patterns in arithmetic.	
Math.3.OA.B.8 Solve two–step word problems using the four operations. Represent these problems using equations with a letter standing for the unknown quantity. Assess the reasonableness of answers using mental computation and estimation strategies including rounding.	29–30, 33–36, 37–40, 45–48, 49–52
Number & Operations in Base Ten	
Use place value understanding and properties of operations to perform multi–digit arithmetic.	
Math.3.NBT.A.1 Use place value understanding to round whole numbers to the nearest 10 or 100.	41–44, 45–48
Math.3.NBT.A.2 Fluently add and subtract within 1,000 using strategies and algorithms based on place value, properties of operations, and/or the relationship between addition and subtraction.	1–4
Math.3.NBT.A.3 Multiply one–digit whole numbers by multiples of 10 in the range 10–90 (e.g., 9 × 80, 5 × 60) using strategies based on place value and properties of operations.	49–52
Number & Operations—Fractions	
Develop understanding of fractions as numbers.	
Math.3.NF.A.2 Understand a fraction as a number on the number line; represent fractions on a number line diagram.	53–56
Math.3.NF.A.2a Represent a fraction 1/*b* on a number line diagram by defining the interval from 0 to 1 as the whole and partitioning it into *b* equal parts. Recognize that each part has size 1/*b* and that the endpoint of the part based at 0 locates the number 1/*b* on the number line.	53–56
Math.3.NF.A.3 Explain equivalence of fractions in special cases, and compare fractions by reasoning about their size.	57–60

Number & Operations—Fractions *(cont.)*	Problem #s
Math.3.NF.A.3a Understand two fractions as equivalent (equal) if they are the same size, or the same point on a number line.	57–60
Math.3.NF.A.3b Recognize and generate simple equivalent fractions, e.g., 1/2 = 2/4, 4/6 = 2/3). Explain why the fractions are equivalent, e.g., by using a visual fraction model.	57–60
Math.3.NF.A.3c Express whole numbers as fractions, and recognize fractions that are equivalent to whole numbers. *Examples: Express 3 in the form 3 = 3/1; recognize that 6/1 = 6; locate 4/4 and 1 at the same point of a number line diagram.*	61–64

Measurement & Data	
Solve problems involving measurement and estimation.	
Math.3.MD.A.1 Tell and write time to the nearest minute and measure time intervals in minutes. Solve word problems involving addition and subtraction of time intervals in minutes, e.g., by representing the problem on a number line diagram.	73–76, 77–80, 81–84, 85–88
Math.3.MD.A.2 Measure and estimate liquid volumes and masses of objects using standard units of grams (g), kilograms (kg), and liters (l). Add, subtract, multiply, or divide to solve one-step word problems involving masses or volumes that are given in the same units, e.g., by using drawings (such as a beaker with a measurement scale) to represent the problem.	65–68
Represent and interpret data.	
Math.3.MD.B.3 Draw a scaled picture graph and a scaled bar graph to represent a data set with several categories. Solve one- and two-step "how many more" and "how many less" problems using information presented in scaled bar graphs. *For example, draw a bar graph in which each square in the bar graph might represent 5 pets.*	5–8, 9–12
Geometric measurement: understand concepts of area and relate area to multiplication and to addition.	
Math.3.MD.C.5 Recognize area as an attribute of plane figures and understand concepts of area measurement.	93–96
Math.3.MD.C.7 Relate area to the operations of multiplication and addition.	93–96
Geometric measurement: recognize perimeter.	
Math.3.MD.D.8 Solve real world and mathematical problems involving perimeters of polygons, including finding the perimeter given the side lengths, finding an unknown side length, and exhibiting rectangles with the same perimeter and different areas or with the same area and different perimeters.	89–92, 97–100

Geometry	
Reason with shapes and their attributes.	
Math.3.G.A.1 Understand that shapes in different categories (e.g., rhombuses, rectangles, and others) may share attributes (e.g., having four sides), and that the shared attributes can define a larger category (e.g., quadrilaterals). Recognize rhombuses, rectangles, and squares as examples of quadrilaterals, and draw examples of quadrilaterals that do not belong to any of these subcategories.	69–72

Test A　　Name: _____

Directions: Read the word problem carefully. Select the best answer for each question.

Sarah's class is doing a project about land features. The children need to bring in 24 blue markers to color the sky. Sarah is bringing in 6 blue markers. How many more blue markers will the class need to color the sky?

1. What fact will help you solve this word problem?

    A. Sarah is doing a project.

    B. Sarah needs markers.

    C. Sarah is bringing in 6 blue markers.

    D. The class will be coloring the sky.

    > A *fact* is information that is needed to solve the problem.

2. What clue words help you decide what operation is needed to solve the problem?

    A. how many

    B. how many more

    C. need to color

    D. bring in 24 markers

    > *Clue words* give you a hint about how to solve the problem.

3. What operation will you use to solve this word problem?

    A. addition

    B. multiplication

    C. subtraction

    D. division

    > Think about it. You know the total number of markers and the number of markers Sarah is bringing to class. How do you find the answer?

4. What is the answer to the word problem?

    A. 48 markers

    B. 30 markers

    C. 12 markers

    D. 18 markers

    SHOW YOUR WORK!

    > Does your choice make sense? Is it less than the total number of markers needed?

| Test A | Name: _____ |

Directions: Look at the bar graph carefully. Select the best answer for each question.

Four third-grade classes wanted to find out which fruit most children like to eat. The classes decided to vote to find out. After the vote, they tallied the results and put the data on the bar graph below.

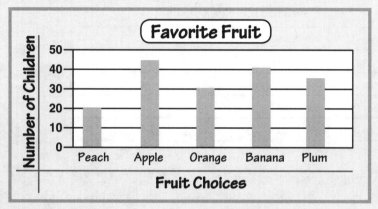

5. Which fruit received the most votes?

   A. orange

   B. peach

   C. apple

   D. banana

6. How many people liked the plum the best?

   A. 30

   B. 40

   C. 32

   D. 35

7. Which fruit had twice as many votes as the peach?

   A. apple

   B. banana

   C. orange

   D. plum

8. What is the difference between the greatest and the least number of votes?

   A. 25

   B. 65

   C. 20

   D. 15

SHOW YOUR WORK!

Bar graphs use bars set along a scale to represent data. The taller the bar, the greater the amount that bar represents.

Examine the bar for plum. The bar is between two lines on the scale, so the amount is between those two amounts.

Think about the meaning of *twice*. If someone has one thing and you have *twice* as many, how many would you have?

The clue word *difference* means that you should subtract.

Test A   Name: _____

Directions: Look at the pictograph carefully. Select the best answer for each question.

An ice-cream company asked 40 children to name their favorite ice-cream flavors. The pictograph below shows the results of that survey.

Key: 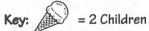 = 2 Children

Favorite Ice Cream	
Flavors	**Number of Votes**
Chocolate	🍦 🍦 🍦 🍦 🍦 🍦
Vanilla	🍦 🍦 🍦 🍦
Strawberry	🍦 🍦
Chocolate Chip	🍦 🍦 🍦 🍦 🍦 🍦 🍦 🍦

9. How many children chose vanilla ice cream as their favorite?

   A. 4

   B. 2

   C. 8

   D. 5

> Pictographs use pictures or symbols to represent data. The key shows the amount represented by each picture.

10. What ice-cream flavor was chosen by four more children than chocolate?

   A. vanilla

   B. strawberry

   C. chocolate chip

   D. none

> Check the key to find out what each ice-cream cone represents. One cone equals two children.

11. If there was only half a cone on the pictograph, what would that mean?

   A. Someone ate the other half.

   B. It stands for 1 child.

   C. It stands for 2 children.

   D. It means a child was not sure what flavor he liked.

> When you see half of a picture, it stands for half the amount.

12. How many children liked strawberry and chocolate ice cream in all?

   A. 16

   B. 12

   C. 8

   D. 20

> Think about the clue words *in all*. *In all* means to find the sum.

Test A   Name: _____

Directions: Read the word problem carefully. Select the best answer for each question.

Nine groups of people went on a fishing trip. There were 3 people in each group. How many people went on the fishing trip all together?

13. What facts do you need to know to solve this problem?

    A. People are going on a fishing trip.

    B. There are 9 groups with 3 people in each group.

    C. There are 9 groups of people.

    D. 3 people are in each group.

> A *fact* is information that is given in the problem.

14. What clue words help you decide what operation is needed to solve the problem?

    A. nine groups

    B. how many

    C. all together

    D. 3 groups

> A *clue word* is a word or phrase found in the question that gives you a hint about how to solve the problem.

15. What operation will you use to solve this word problem?

    A. subtraction

    B. addition

    C. multiplication

    D. division

> Think about it. You know the number of groups and how many people are in each group. How do you find the answer?

16. What is the answer to the word problem?

    A. 12 people

    B. 6 people

    C. 3 people

    D. 27 people

SHOW YOUR WORK!

> Point to the answer. Does it make sense?

Test A   Name: _____

Directions: Read the word problem carefully. Select the best answer for each question.

Julia bought a new sticker book. She has 16 stickers. She wants to put an equal number of stickers on each of the first 4 pages in the sticker book. How many stickers will she put on each page?

17. What information do you need to know to solve this problem?

    A. Julia bought a new sticker book for her stickers, and she has 16 stickers.

    B. Julia has 16 stickers.

    C. She wants to put an equal number of stickers on the first 4 pages.

    D. Julia has 16 stickers, and she wants to put an equal number of stickers on the first 4 pages.

> Read all the answer choices; this will help you choose the *best* answer.

18. What operation should you use when you see the clue words *an equal number of*?

    A. subtraction

    B. addition

    C. division

    D. multiplication

> Think about the meaning of an *equal number of*. If you want to split a quantity into an equal number of groups, what do you do?

19. Which number sentence can be used to solve the word problem?

    A. $16 \times 4 =$

    B. $16 + 4 =$

    C. $16 - 4 =$

    D. $16 \div 4 =$

> Use the process of elimination to help you choose the correct number sentence.

20. What is the answer to the word problem?

    A. 20 stickers

    B. 64 stickers

    C. 4 stickers

    D. 12 stickers

SHOW YOUR WORK!

> Compare your answer to the other answer choices. Does your answer make sense?

Test A   Name: _____

Directions: Read each problem carefully and select the best answer.

21. Which division fact is related to 3 x 6 = 18?

    A. $18 \div 6 = 4$

    B. $18 \div 3 = 6$

    C. $6 \div 3 = 2$

    D. $18 \div 6 = 6$

> Related multiplication and division facts contain the same three numbers.

22. What number completes these related number facts?

    A. 8

    B. 36

    C. 9

    D. 4

$$4 \times \underline{\quad} = 32$$
$$32 \div 4 = \underline{\quad}$$

> Think about the meaning of a *related* fact. What number makes sense in *both* equations?

23. Which related fact would help you solve 56 ÷ 8 = 7?

    A. $56 \times 8 = 7$

    B. $7 + 8 = 15$

    C. $8 \times 7 = 56$

    D. $56 - 8 = 48$

> Remember, multiplication is related to division. Pay attention to the numbers in the equations and the operation being used.

24. What fact does not belong in the same fact family as 5 x 7 = 35?

    A. $35 \div 5 = 7$

    B. $7 \times 5 = 35$

    C. $7 + 5 = 12$

    D. $35 \div 7 = 5$

> Point to each equation. Did you find an equation that does not contain the same numbers as 5 x 7 = 35?

Test A   Name: _____

Directions: Read each word problem carefully. Select the best answer for each question.

Melissa has 3 dogs. She bought 21 dog treats for them. She wants to give each dog the same number of treats. How many treats will each dog get?

25. What clue word helps you decide which operation to use to solve the problem?

   A. has 3 dogs

   B. each

   C. how many

   D. bought dog treats

> The clue word in this problem means that you should divide.

26. Which equation shows the solution for the problem?

   A. 21 x 3 = 63

   B. 24 ÷ 3 = 8

   C. 21 − 3 = 18

   D. 21 ÷ 3 = 7

> Find the total number of dog treats and how many dogs Melissa has. Remember, Melissa wants to *share* the treats *equally* between her 3 dogs.

Willow bought 4 pages of butterfly stickers. On each page there are 9 stickers. How many stickers does Willow have all together?

27. What information do you need to know to solve this problem?

   A. 9 stickers

   B. on each page

   C. 4 pages and 9 stickers on each page

   D. 4 pages and 9 stickers

> Eliminate choices that do not contain enough information to solve the problem.

28. What is the answer to the word problem?

   A. 13 stickers

   B. 5 stickers

   C. 18 stickers

   D. 36 stickers

SHOW YOUR WORK!

> You know there are 4 pages of stickers, and there are 9 stickers on each page. The phrase *all together* is a clue about how to solve the problem.

Test A   Name: _____

Directions: Read each problem carefully and select the best answer.

29. Drew bought a small pizza for $5.49 and a soda for $1.69. He gave the cashier $10. How much change did he get back?

    A. $7.18

    B. $1.82

    C. $2.82

    D. $3.92

    SHOW YOUR WORK!

    Add to find Drew's total, then subtract to find the change.

30. Every day Marco earns $3.00 for walking the neighbor's dog and another $5.00 for delivering newspapers. How much money does he earn in one week?

    A. $40.00

    B. $21.00

    C. $35.00

    D. $56.00

    SHOW YOUR WORK!

    There are seven days in one week.

31. The clerk at the corner bakery puts 6 cookies in each bag. How many cookies will she need to fill 9 bags?

    A. 3 cookies

    B. 15 cookies

    C. 48 cookies

    D. 54 cookies

    SHOW YOUR WORK!

    Remember, multiplication is like repeated addition.

32. Mike jogged a total of 12 miles in 4 days. He jogged an equal amount of miles each day. How many miles did he jog on day one?

    A. 16 miles

    B. 3 miles

    C. 8 miles

    D. 48 miles

    SHOW YOUR WORK!

    Think about the meaning of *an equal amount of.* If you want to split a total number into an equal number of groups, what do you do?

Test A   Name: _____

Directions: Read the multiple-step problem carefully. Select the best answer for each question.

Jake's mom gave him $45 to spend on clothes for school. He paid $12 for a shirt, $19 for pants, and $8 for a belt. How much did Jake spend in all for his school clothes? How much money did Jake have left?

33. What clue helps you know the operation to use to find how much Jake spent?

   A. in all

   B. how much

   C. have left

   D. gave him $45

> The clue to finding how much Jake spent tells you to *add*.

34. What is the answer to the first question?

   A. $31

   B. $39

   C. $20

   D. $84

SHOW YOUR WORK!

> Go back to the problem. Make sure you find the sum of everything that Jake bought.

35. What two facts do you need to know to find how much money Jake had left?

   A. the cost of the pants and the cost of the shirt

   B. the total cost of what Jake bought and how much money he had to spend

   C. Jake had $45 to spend, and he spent $20 for a shirt and a belt.

   D. Jake still needs to buy a hat, and he had $45 to spend on clothes.

> *Have left* means to find the difference between two numbers. Think about what two amounts you would need to subtract to find how much money Jake has left.

36. What is the answer to the second question?

   A. $84

   B. $14

   C. $25

   D. $6

SHOW YOUR WORK!

> Use the answer from the first question to answer the second question.

Test A | Name: _____

Directions: Read the multiple-step problem carefully. Select the best answer for each question.

There are 58 children taking a trip to the zoo. They form 6 groups with 8 children in each group. The rest of the children form another group. How many children are left to be in that group?

37. What is the hidden question in this problem?
    A. How many children are going to the zoo?
    B. What is the difference between the number of groups and the number of children in each group?
    C. How many children are in the 6 groups in all?
    D. How many children are in each group?

> What do you need to know before you can find how many children are left after the 6 groups are formed?

38. What equation could be used to answer the hidden question?
    A. $6 \times 8 = n$
    B. $58 - 8 = n$
    C. $6 + 8 = n$
    D. $8 - 6 = n$

> What operation would you use to find the *total number* of things in *equal groups?*

39. What clue in the question helps you know which operation to use to finish solving?
    A. in that group
    B. how many children
    C. how many
    D. are left

> The clue words in this problem tell you to find the *difference* between two numbers.

40. What is the answer to the problem?
    A. 10 groups
    B. 48 children
    C. 10 children
    D. 50 children

    SHOW YOUR WORK!

> Use the answer from the hidden question to solve the problem.

Test A | Name: _____

Directions: Read each problem carefully and select the best answer.

41. Round 16 to the nearest ten.

- **A.** 17
- **B.** 10
- **C.** 26
- **D.** 20

> Find the digit in the tens place before you try to solve the problem.

42. Which number, when rounded to the hundreds place, is 500?

- **A.** 559
- **B.** 464
- **C.** 449
- **D.** 560

> Look *one place to the right* of the place you want to round to. Is the number 5 or greater? If so, round up.

43. Round 871 to the nearest hundred.

- **A.** 870
- **B.** 880
- **C.** 900
- **D.** 800

> Remember, if you round up, replace all the digits to the right with zeros and add 1 to the number in the place you want to round to.

44. What is 67,345 rounded to nearest thousand?

- **A.** 67,300
- **B.** 70,000
- **C.** 68,000
- **D.** 67,000

> Pay attention to the number *one place to the right* of the place you are rounding to.

Test A	**Name:** _____

Directions: Read each problem carefully and select the best answer.

45. Round each number to the nearest ten and then add.

A. 87
B. 80
C. 90
D. 85

> 45 + 42

> Remember to find the digit in the tens place and check the number to the right of it. If the number to the right is 5 or greater, round up.

46. Which addition problem has a sum of about 80 when rounded to the nearest ten?

A. 79 + 10
B. 69 + 20
C. 45 + 46
D. 35 + 35

SHOW YOUR WORK!

> Round each number and then find each sum to find the correct answer.

47. Round each number to the nearest hundred and then add.

A. 910
B. 800
C. 900
D. 950

> 365 + 545

> Point to the numbers in the hundreds places; these are the numbers that you are asked to round.

48. Sandy and Helen sold candy bars for a local girls' club. Sandy sold 155 candy bars, and Helen sold 125 candy bars. To the nearest hundred, about how many candy bars did they sell all together?

A. about 290 candy bars
B. about 300 candy bars
C. about 330 candy bars
D. about 200 candy bars

SHOW YOUR WORK!

> The word *about* is a clue that indicates you must estimate to find the answer.

Test A   Name: _____

Directions: Read each problem carefully and select the best answer.

49. Estimate the product by rounding the first factor to the nearest ten.

   A. 90

   B. 120

   C. 114

   D. 160

   38 x 3

> Look to the right of the number you are rounding. If that number is 5 or greater, round up; if that number is less than 5, round down.

50. Estimate the product by rounding the second factor to the nearest ten.

   A. 260

   B. 240

   C. 280

   D. 270

   4 x 65

> Think about it: the *greatest* factor in the problem should be rounded to make it easier to estimate the product.

51. Which problem has a product of about 150?

   A. 64 x 5

   B. 75 x 4

   C. 45 x 3

   D. 55 x 2

> Remember to round the greatest factor to the nearest ten before multiplying.

52. If you estimate the products of 71 x 6 and 65 x 6 by rounding each two-digit number to the nearest ten, is it possible for the estimates to be the same?

   A. No. 71 is greater than 65, so the estimates would not be the same.

   B. Yes. 71 rounded to the nearest ten is 70 and 65 rounded to the nearest ten is 70. Both are multiplied by 6, so the estimates would be the same.

   C. No. Since 71 rounds down to 70 and 65 rounds down to 60, it would not be possible to have the same estimate.

   D. Yes. 71 rounded to the nearest ten is 60 and 65 rounded to the nearest ten is 60. Both are multiplied by 6, so the estimates would be the same.

> Pay attention! Which factors can be rounded up? Rounded down?

Test A | Name: _____

Directions: Read each problem carefully and select the best answer.

---

53. What fraction is represented by the dot on the number line?

A. $\frac{3}{4}$

B. $\frac{1}{2}$

C. $\frac{3}{5}$

D. $\frac{5}{6}$

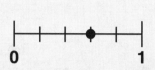

> Remember to count the number of segments between 0 and 1 to find the denominator. Then count the number of segments between 0 and the dot to find the numerator.

54. What fraction of the shape is shaded?

A. $\frac{1}{4}$

B. $\frac{1}{2}$

C. $\frac{3}{6}$

D. $\frac{3}{4}$

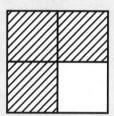

> Count the total number of equal parts to find the denominator. Then count the number of shaded parts to find the numerator.

55. Vicki made one dozen (12) chocolate cupcakes. She put sprinkles on 7 of the cupcakes. What fraction of the cupcakes has sprinkles?

A. $\frac{5}{12}$

B. $\frac{1}{7}$

C. $\frac{7}{12}$

D. $\frac{1}{12}$

> Think about how many cupcakes have sprinkles and how many cupcakes there are in all.

56. Mr. Walker picks eight tomatoes from his garden. Five of the tomatoes are green and three of the tomatoes are red. What fraction represents the number of red tomatoes?

A. $\frac{1}{8}$

B. $\frac{3}{8}$

C. $\frac{3}{5}$

D. $\frac{5}{8}$

> Mr. Walker picked 8 tomatoes all together. How many were red?

Test A　　Name: _____

Directions: Read each problem carefully and select the best answer.

57. Which fraction is the greatest?

A.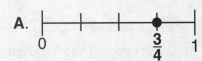
$\frac{3}{4}$

B.
$\frac{5}{6}$

C.
$\frac{1}{3}$

D. The fractions are all equal.

> Which dot is closest to 1?

58. Which fraction is the least?

A. 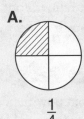　B. 　C. 　D.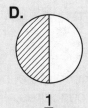

$\frac{1}{4}$　　$\frac{2}{3}$　　$\frac{2}{6}$　　$\frac{1}{2}$

> Look at the shapes. Compare the shaded areas of the circles.

59. What is the missing number that makes these two fractions equal?

A. 4
B. 8
C. 12
D. 2

$$\frac{4}{8} = \frac{1}{\square}$$

> Use what you know to *simplify* (reduce) the fraction.

60. Which fraction is equivalent to $\frac{1}{4}$?

A. $\frac{2}{8}$
B. $\frac{1}{3}$
C. $\frac{1}{2}$
D. $\frac{6}{8}$

> Remember to reduce each fraction to its simplest form before comparing them.

Test A   Name: _____

Directions: Read each problem carefully and select the best answer.

61. Which fraction is equivalent to 3?

A. $\frac{3}{3}$

B. $\frac{3}{1}$

C. $\frac{1}{3}$

D. none of the above

> Remember that fractions represent division. Which fraction results in a quotient of 3 when the numerator is divided by the denominator?

62. Which fraction equals 1?

A. $\frac{6}{1}$

B. $\frac{1}{6}$

C. $\frac{6}{6}$

D. $\frac{2}{1}$

> Remember that a fraction that equals the whole number 1 has the same denominator and numerator.

63. What is another way to express $\frac{12}{12}$?

A. $\frac{1}{12}$

B. 12

C. 1

D. $\frac{12}{12}$

> Remember that the fraction bar means division.

64. Which number line shows a fraction that is equal to 1?

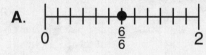

A.

0    $\frac{6}{6}$ 2

B.

0    $\frac{4}{4}$ 2

C.

0    $\frac{7}{7}$ 2

> Compare to help you find the answer.

D. all of the above

Test A | Name: _____

Directions: Read each problem carefully and select the best answer.

65. Which is the best estimate for the weight of a bike?

A. 10 g

B. 2 kg

C. 14 kg

D. 100 g

A paperclip weighs about 1 g (gram). A baseball bat weighs about 1 kg (kilogram).

66. Which is the best estimate for the capacity of a fishbowl?

A. 4 mL

B. 500 L

C. 700 mL

D. 3 L

One drop of liquid is about 1 mL (milliliter). Four cups of liquid is about 1 L (liter).

67. Which is the best unit to measure the capacity of a swimming pool?

A. liters

B. kilograms

C. milliliters

D. grams

Capacity is the amount of liquid a container can hold.

68. Charlie has a box of business cards. Each business card weighs about 1 gram. The entire box weighs 2 kilograms. How many business cards are in a box?

A. 1,000 business cards

B. 200 business cards

C. 2,000 business cards

D. 100 business cards

SHOW YOUR WORK!

Remember: 1,000 grams = 1 kilogram.

Test A	Name: _____

Directions: Read each problem carefully and select the best answer.

69. Is this shape a polygon?

   A. No, one side is shorter than the other.

   B. Yes, it is a closed shape made of line segments.

   C. No, it should have a curved side.

   D. Yes, it has two parallel sides.

> Polygons are closed, two-dimensional shapes. They are made with straight lines.

70. How many fewer sides does a hexagon have than an octagon?

   A. fourteen

   B. eight

   C. two

   D. six

> A hexagon has six sides. An octagon has eight sides. The word *fewer* is a clue to subtract.

71. How is a scalene triangle different from an isosceles triangle?

   A. No sides are the same length on a scalene triangle, but at least two sides are the same length on an isosceles triangle.

   B. There is a right angle on a scalene triangle, but an isosceles triangle does not have a right angle.

   C. All the angles on a scalene triangle are different, but the angles on an isosceles triangle are always the same.

   D. A scalene triangle has two long sides and one short side, but an isosceles triangle has no equal sides.

> The sides on a *scalene triangle* are all different lengths. An *isosceles triangle* has two or three sides that are the same length.

72. What is the name of this shape?

   A. quadrilateral

   B. hexagon

   C. triangle

   D. pentagon

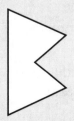

> Point to the shape and count each side. Remember, a polygon is named by how many sides it has.

Test A	Name: _____

Directions: Read each problem carefully and select the best answer.

73. What two ways can you say the time on this clock?

   A. 6:15 and 15 minutes to 6

   B. three thirty and half past 3

   C. 15 minutes after 6 and quarter after 6

   D. quarter after 3 and 3:15

> Look carefully at the clock hands. The hour hand is shorter than the minute hand.

74. The movie started at 8:30. Marie got to the theater at quarter to 9. Was she late?

   A. Yes, Marie was 15 minutes late.

   B. Yes, Marie was 30 minutes late.

   C. No, Marie was 15 minutes early.

   D. Yes, Marie was 45 minutes late.

> Quarter to 9 is the same as 8:45.

75. What answer does not represent the time on this clock?

   A. quarter to 11

   B. 11:45

   C. quarter to 12

   D. 15 minutes to 12

> The minute hand on the 9 means there are 15 minutes until the next hour.

76. Where are the hands on a clock that show 1:30?

   A. The hour hand is on the 1. The minute hand is on the 6.

   B. The hour hand is halfway between the 1 and 2. The minute hand is on the 6.

   C. The hour hand is on the 6. The minute hand is on the 1.

   D. The hour hand is between the 1 and 2. The minute hand is between the 5 and 6.

> There are sixty minutes in an hour. Thirty minutes is half of sixty, so the minute hand would be halfway around.

Test A   Name: _____

Directions: Read each problem carefully and select the best answer.

77. What time is shown on the clock?

    A. half past 5

    B. 5:28

    C. 6:28

    D. twenty-eight minutes to 5

Count by fives until you get to the 5 on the clock. Then add 3 more minutes.

78. Michael went to the library at 6:41. What is another way to say that time?

    A. twenty minutes to 7

    B. nineteen minutes to 6

    C. nineteen minutes to 7

    D. forty-one minutes to 6

The hour hand is moving toward the 7. Count how many minutes it is until seven o'clock.

79. Cindy and her family went out to dinner. They were at the restaurant for 1 hour and 38 minutes. How many minutes were Cindy and her family at the restaurant in all?

    A. 38 minutes

    B. 39 minutes

    C. 22 minutes

    D. 98 minutes

SHOW YOUR WORK!

Remember, there are sixty minutes in an hour.

80. Krystle started to practice the piano at the time shown on the clock. What time did Krystle start to practice?

    A. one fifty-one

    B. ten minutes to one

    C. two fifty-one

    D. seven minutes after ten

The minute hand is not exactly on the 10. Count by fives and then add 1 more minute.

Test A   Name: _____

Directions: Read each problem carefully and select the best answer for each question.

81. Max started hockey practice at 3:30 p.m. The practice ended at 6:00 p.m. How long was Max's hockey practice?

    A. one hour and thirty minutes

    B. three hours

    C. two hours and thirty minutes

    D. two hours

    > Begin at the starting time. Count the hours and then the minutes.

82. Juan finished his homework at 4:00 p.m. For homework, he read about rocks and minerals for 25 minutes. He also studied spelling for 15 minutes. What time did Juan start his homework?

    A. 4:40 p.m.

    B. 3:20 p.m.

    C. 3:35 p.m.

    D. 3:45 p.m.

    > Add the time Juan took to do his reading and spelling homework. Then move backward that number of minutes on a clock, starting at 4:00.

83. Stephanie got to the carnival at the time shown on the clock. She left 5 hours and 10 minutes later. What time did Stephanie leave the carnival?

    A. 7:00

    B. 6:10

    C. 3:10

    D. 7:10

    > Look at the time on the clock. Go forward 5 hours. Now add 10 minutes.

84. Lily went to bed at 8:00 p.m. She woke up at 7:15 a.m. to go to school. How long did Lily sleep?

    A. 11 hours and 15 minutes

    B. 7 hours and 15 minutes

    C. 45 minutes

    D. 11 hours

    > Draw a picture of a clock. Start at 8:00. Touch each number as you count the hours until you get to 7. Don't forget to add the minutes.

Test A   Name: _____

Directions: Read each problem carefully and select the best answer.

85. The Cook family drove 5 hours to get to New York. How many minutes did the family drive?

A. 12 minutes

B. 150 minutes

C. 60 minutes

D. 300 minutes

SHOW YOUR WORK!

1 hour = 60 minutes
To change hours into minutes, multiply by 60.

86. Charlie practiced his part for the play for 4 weeks. How many days did Charlie practice?

A. 14 days

B. 20 days

C. 28 days

D. 7 days

SHOW YOUR WORK!

1 week = 7 days
Change weeks into days by multiplying by 7.

87. Jessica went to camp for 3 weeks and 3 days. How many days did Jessica go to camp?

A. 24 days

B. 21 days

C. 17 days

D. 3 days

SHOW YOUR WORK!

Multiply to find how many days in three weeks. Then add 3 days.

88. On Monday, Carol read about the solar system for 1 hour and 10 minutes. On Wednesday, she read about stars for 85 minutes. Which day did Carol read longer?

A. Carol read 10 minutes longer on Monday.

B. Carol read 15 minutes longer on Wednesday.

C. Carol read the same amount of time on both days.

D. Carol read 15 minutes longer on Monday.

SHOW YOUR WORK!

First, find the total number of minutes Carol read on Monday. Then compare the minutes for the two days.

Test A   Name: _____

Directions: Read each problem carefully and select the best answer.

89. What is the perimeter of the figure?

A. 20 in.

B. 31 ft.

C. 18 in.

D. 31 in.

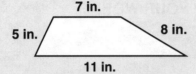

> Find the perimeter by adding all the sides.

90. What is the perimeter of this *regular* polygon?

A. 28 cm

B. 7 cm

C. 21 cm

D. 49 cm

7 cm

> This regular polygon is a *square* with four equal sides. Add the lengths of all four sides of the square to find the perimeter.

91. The shape of the soccer field is a rectangle. The field is 50 feet long and 25 feet wide. What is the perimeter of the soccer field?

A. 75 ft.

B. 150 ft.

C. 100 ft.

D. 125 ft.

> Draw a picture of the rectangular soccer field. Label each side. Then add the lengths of all four sides.

92. Which pair of figures has the same perimeter?

A.

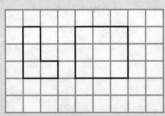

B.

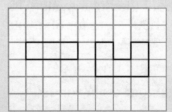

> As you count each side of the shape, mark it with your pencil. Write the perimeter next to the shape.

C.

D.

Test A   Name: _____

Directions: Read each problem carefully and select the best answer.

93. What is the area of the figure when ☐ = 1 square unit.

   A. 14 sq. units

   B. 20 sq. units

   C. 16 sq. units

   D. 18 sq. units

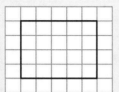

> Count all the squares to find the area.

94. What is the area of this rectangle?

   A. 24 sq. ft.

   B. 12 sq. ft.

   C. 8 ft.

   D. 32 sq. ft.

8 ft.

4 ft.

> Area is length x width.

95. What is the area of a polygon that is 7 inches long and 6 inches wide?

   A. 42 in.

   B. 13 sq. in.

   C. 42 sq. in.

   D. 26 in.

SHOW YOUR WORK!

> Draw the polygon and label the measurement of each side. Now, multiply the length by the width.

96. What is the area of the figure?

   A. 20 sq. cm

   B. 24 sq. cm

   C. 35 sq. cm

   D. 14 sq. cm

2 cm

3 cm

5 cm   **5 cm**

2 cm

7 cm

> Divide the figure into two rectangles. Find the area of each rectangle, and then add the two areas together to find the area of the entire figure.

Test A   Name: _____

Directions: Read each problem carefully and select the best answer

97. A rectangle has a length of 6 ft. and a width of 4 ft. Which rectangle has the same area?

A.   **B.**   **C.**   **D.**

3 ft.
5 ft.

5 ft.
2 ft.

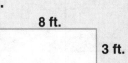
8 ft.
3 ft.

2 ft.
7 ft.

> Area = l x w
> First multiply 6 ft. x 4 ft. to find the area of the original rectangle. Then find the area of each answer choice.

98. A rectangle has an area of 16 sq. cm. What are possible dimensions of the rectangle?

A. length: 7 cm; width: 5 cm

B. length: 8 cm; width: 2 cm

C. length: 6 cm; width: 3 cm

D. length: 5 cm; width: 4 cm

> Draw each rectangle and find the area. Which one has as area of 16 sq. cm?

99. What is the greatest possible perimeter of a rectangle with an area of 32 sq. ft.?

A. length: 32 ft.; width: 1 ft.

B. length: 8 ft.; width: 4 ft.

C. length: 16 ft.; width: 2 ft.

D. length: 6 ft.; width: 5 ft.

> Perimeter = (2 x l) + (2 x w)
> Find the perimeter for each rectangle.

100. Which figure has the same perimeter as a rectangle with a length of 7 yd. and a width of 4 yd.?

> $P = (2 \times l) + (2 \times w)$

A.
6 yd.
3 yd.

B.
8 yd.
2 yd.

C.
2 yd.
9 yd.

D.
28 yd.
1 yd.

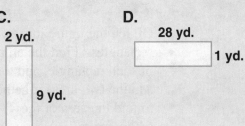

SHOW YOUR WORK!

Test B   Name: _____

Directions: Read the word problem carefully. Select the best answer for each question.

The bakery opens at 9 a.m. every day. The owner baked 144 chocolate cupcakes and 275 vanilla cupcakes. How many cupcakes did the owner bake all together?

1. What information do you need to know to solve the problem?

    A. There are chocolate and vanilla cupcakes.

    B. The bakery opens at 9:00 in the morning.

    C. The owner baked more vanilla cupcakes than chocolate cupcakes.

    D. There are 144 chocolate cupcakes and 275 vanilla cupcakes.

2. What operation should you use when you see the clue phrase *all together*?

    A. subtraction

    B. addition

    C. multiplication

    D. division

> *All together* is a clue that means to find the sum.

3. If the bakery opened at 10:00, would the answer to the problem be different?

    A. No, the number of cupcakes is the same.

    B. Yes, the baker would not have time to bake as many cupcakes.

    C. Yes, because 10:00 is one hour later than 9:00.

    D. No, because the baker will work harder to bake all the cupcakes.

> Think about it. Do you need to know what time the bakery opens in order to solve the problem?

4. What is the answer to the word problem?

    A. 428 cupcakes

    B. 419 cupcakes

    C. 131 cupcakes

    D. 319 cupcakes

SHOW YOUR WORK!

Test B   Name: _____

Directions: Look at the bar graph carefully. Select the best answer for each question.

Justin wanted to know what sport was the most popular in his school. He interviewed the children and tallied the results. Justin displayed the data on the bar graph below.

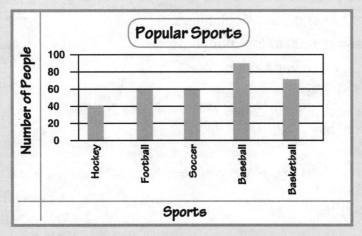

5. What sport was chosen by exactly 40 students?

   A. soccer   **C**. hockey

   B. baseball   **D**. football

6. How does the scale increase on this bar graph?

   A. increases by 10

   B. increases by 5

   C. increases by 100

   D. increases by 20

   > The *scale* on this bar graph is the numbers on the side from 0 to 100.

7. What is the total number of people who chose football and baseball?

   A. 140 people

   B. 30 people

   C. 145 people

   D. 150 people

   > **SHOW YOUR WORK!**

8. Which statement is true?

   A. Soccer and basketball were chosen by the same number of people.

   B. More people chose football than hockey and basketball combined.

   C. More people chose football than baseball.

   D. Twenty more people liked soccer than hockey.

   > Read each statement before you select the answer. Use process of elimination until you find the best answer.

Test B　　Name: _____

Directions: Look at the pictograph carefully.　Select the best answer for each question.

Mrs. Cook's third grade class had a car wash to raise money for a class trip.　The car wash was held for four days.　The class tallied the car wash results and created the pictograph below.

Key: 🚗 = 4 Cars

Car Wash	
Days	**Number of Cars Washed**
Thursday	🚗 🚗 🚗
Friday	🚗 🚗 🚗
Saturday	🚗 🚗 🚗 🚗 🚗
Sunday	🚗 🚗 🚗

9. On what two days were the same number of cars washed?

   A. Thursday and Friday　　**C.** Thursday and Sunday

   B. Sunday and Friday　　　**D.** none

10. How many cars were washed on Saturday?

   A. 18 cars　　**C.** 20 cars

   B. 4 ½ cars　　**D.** 16 cars

   ⟨ Remember that 🚗 represents half of four cars washed. ⟩

11. What is the difference between the greatest and the least number of cars washed?

   A. 2 cars　　**C.** 7 cars

   B. 28 cars　　**D.** 8 cars

12. Which statement is false?

   A. All together, there were 24 cars washed on Friday and Sunday.

   B. The least amount of cars washed was on Thursday.

   C. The combined number of cars washed on Thursday and Friday was equal to the number that was washed on Saturday.

   D. Each 🚗 on the pictograph represents four actual cars washed.

   ⟨ Go back to the pictograph. Review the information in each sentence before you make your answer choice. ⟩

Test B   Name: _____

Directions: Read the word problem carefully. Select the best answer for each question.

Nicole decided to bake chocolate chip cookies for the holidays. Each batch of cookie dough makes 12 cookies. If she makes 4 batches of chocolate chip cookie dough, how many cookies will she bake in all?

13. What information do you need to know to solve this problem?

A. Nicole decides to bake chocolate chip cookies.

B. Nicole will make 4 batches of cookies for the holidays.

C. Each batch of chocolate chip cookie dough that Nicole prepares will make 12 cookies.

D. Each batch of cookie dough makes 12 cookies, and Nicole will make 4 batches of dough.

14. What clue helps you decide what operation is needed to solve the problem?

A. decides to bake

B. in all

C. each batch

D. make 4 batches

> A clue is a word or phrase found in a question that gives you a hint about how to solve the problem.

15. What operation will you use to solve the word problem?

A. addition

B. subtraction

C. division

D. multiplication

> You know that one batch of cookie dough makes 12 cookies, and Nicole is making 4 batches. How do you find the answer?

16. What is the answer to the word problem?

A. 16 cookies

B. 8 cookies

C. 48 cookies

D. 3 cookies

SHOW YOUR WORK!

Test B   Name: _____

Directions: Read the word problem carefully. Select the best answer for each question.

On Saturday, Andrew went to a baseball game. There are 9 innings in a baseball game. Each team must make 3 outs per inning for a total of 6 outs per inning. If 18 outs have been made in a game, how many innings have been played?

17. What two facts do you need to know to solve this problem?
    A. Six outs must be made in each inning, and a total of 18 outs must be made in a game.
    B. Andrew went to a baseball game, and in a baseball game there must be 6 outs in each inning.
    C. There are 9 innings in a baseball game, and 18 outs have been made so far.
    D. Six outs must be made in each inning, and 18 outs have been made so far.

18. What clue helps you decide what operation is needed to solve the problem?
    A. how many   **C.** there are 3 outs
    B. total of 18 outs   **D.** in each inning

> Remember to look for word clues to help you decide what operation to use.

19. Which math symbol is needed to complete the number sentence that can be used to solve the problem?
    A. +
    B. ÷
    C. −
    D. x

    $$18 \; \square \; 6 = n$$

> You know there are 6 outs in each inning and a total of 18 outs have been made. How do you find the answer?

20. What is the answer to the word problem?
    A. 54 innings
    B. 3 innings
    C. 15 innings
    D. 9 innings

SHOW YOUR WORK!

Test B   Name: _____

Directions: Read each problem carefully and select the best answer.

---

21. 9 x 7 = 63 and 63 ÷ 7 = 9 are two related facts.
What facts would complete this fact family?

   A. 63 ÷ 9 = 7 and 9 + 7 = 16

   B. 9 x 7 = 63 and 9 x 4 = 36

   C. 63 ÷ 9 = 7 and 7 x 9 = 63

   D. 7 x 7 = 49 and 7 x 9 = 63

22. What is the value of *n* in these related facts?

   A. 63

   B. 8

   C. 18

   D. 7

$$3 \times n = 21$$
$$21 \div 3 = n$$

> Equations can contain letters as well as numbers. The letter *n* stands for an unknown number. The unknown number is the number that will make the equation *true*.

23. Are 4 x 3 = 12 and 6 x 2 = 12 related facts?

   A. Yes, the product is 12 for each fact.

   B. No, one fact should be division.

   C. Yes, both facts use multiplication.

   D. No, the three numbers in each equation must be the same.

> Remember, related multiplication and division facts must contain the same three numbers.

24. Jonathan needs 28 pencils. The pencils come in packages of 4. He knows he should divide 28 by 4 to find out how many packages he should buy, but he doesn't know the answer to this division problem. What fact would help Jonathan?

   A. 4 x 7 = 28

   B. 28 – 4 = 24

   C. 4 + 4 + 4 = 12

   D. 4 + 7 = 11

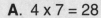

Test B   Name: _____

Directions: Read each word problem carefully. Select the best answer for each question.

There are 6 players on a hockey team. At the skating rink, 8 teams were playing. How many players were at the rink in all?

25. Which addition sentence is equal to 8 x 6?

- **A.** 8 + 8 + 8 + 8 + 8 + 8 + 8 + 8
- **B.** 8 + 6
- **C.** 6 + 6 + 6 + 6 + 6 + 6 + 6 + 6
- **D.** 8 – 6

> 8 x 6 means that there were 8 teams and that there were 6 people on each team.

26. What is the answer to the problem above?

- **A.** 8 x 6 = 48 teams
- **B.** 8 + 6 = 14 players
- **C.** 8 x 6 = 48 players
- **D.** 48 ÷ 6 = 8 players

Richard likes to collect old coins. He collected 81 coins and put them in a coin book. Nine coins fit on each page of his coin book. How many pages of the coin book did Richard fill with coins?

27. What operation would you use to solve this problem?

- **A.** multiplication
- **B.** division
- **C.** addition
- **D.** subtraction

> Think about the facts you know. Richard has 81 coins. He divides the coins equally by putting 9 coins on each page.

28. What is the answer to the word problem?

- **A.** 9 pages
- **B.** 72 pages
- **C.** 90 pages
- **D.** 81 pages

SHOW YOUR WORK!

Test B　　Name: _____

Directions: Read each word problem carefully. Select the best answer for each question.

29. A CD rental program was recently added to the school store. The rental fee is $2.25 per CD. If Michael rents 3 CDs for 1 week and pays with a $10 bill, how much change will he receive?

    A. $6.75
    B. $3.25
    C. $3.75
    D. $4.25

    SHOW YOUR WORK!

    First, find how much Michael paid for the CD's.

30. During the first week of the school book rental program, 120 books were rented. It costs $2 to rent each book. How much money was collected in all during the first week of the rental program?

    A. $60
    B. $122
    C. $240
    D. $118

    SHOW YOUR WORK!

31. Chrissy has a bag with 24 pieces of chocolate candy. She divides the candy equally among 3 friends and herself. How many pieces of candy will each person receive?

    A. 27 pieces of candy
    B. 21 pieces of candy
    C. 8 pieces of candy
    D. 6 pieces of candy

    SHOW YOUR WORK!

    Read carefully. How many people will receive candy?

32. Ava and Bella are friends. Ava has a bag with 12 pieces of chocolate candy, and Bella has a bag with 24 pieces of candy. If Ava and Bella combine their candy into 1 bag and then share the candy equally, how many pieces of candy will each girl get?

    A. 16 pieces
    B. 12 pieces
    C. 6 pieces
    D. 18 pieces

    SHOW YOUR WORK!

Test B　　Name: _____

Directions: Read the word problem carefully. Select the best answer for each question.

Eddie and 3 of his friends each made a meatball sub. Each sub had 3 meatballs on it.   How many meatballs in all did Eddie and his friends use to make the subs? Eddie's brother came in and made himself a sub with 4 meatballs on it. What is the total number of meatballs used to make all the subs?

33. What operation would you use to answer the first question?

   A. addition

   B. subtraction

   C. multiplication

   D. division

34. What equation can be used to answer the first question?

   A. 3 x 3 = 9

   B. 4 x 3 = 12

   C. 3 + 3 = 6

   D. 3 + 4 = 7

> Go back to the word problem. How many people made subs with 3 meatballs—3 or 4?

35. What information is needed to answer the second question in the problem?

   A. Eddie's brother put more meatballs on his sub than the other people.

   B. Eddie and 3 friends made subs.

   C. the total number of meatballs Eddie and his 3 friends had on their subs and the number of meatballs Eddie's brother had on his sub.

   D. the total number of subs made

36. What is the answer to the second question?

   A. 16 subs

   B. 13 meatballs

   C. 13 subs

   D. 16 meatballs

> Use the answer from the first problem to help answer the second question.

SHOW YOUR WORK!

Test B   Name: _____

Directions: Read the word problem carefully. Select the best answer for each question.

Sandy took pictures on her four-day trip to Italy. She took 53 pictures on Monday, 48 pictures on Tuesday, 37 pictures on Wednesday, and 14 more pictures on Thursday than she took on Wednesday. When the trip was over, Sandy deleted 29 pictures. How many pictures does Sandy have now?

37. What is the hidden question in this problem?

    A. How many pictures did Sandy take on Monday, Tuesday, and Wednesday?

    B. How many pictures did Sandy take in all on her four-day trip?

    C. How many more pictures did she take on Monday than she took on Thursday?

    D. How many more pictures can Sandy take?

38. What is the answer to the hidden question?

    A. 152 pictures

    B. 136 pictures

    C. 189 pictures

    D. 181 pictures

SHOW YOUR WORK!

> Think about it. On Thursday, Sandy took 14 *more* pictures than she did on Wednesday. How many pictures did she take on Thursday?

39. What operation would you use to answer the question in the story?

    A. addition

    B. multiplication

    C. division

    D. subtraction

> *Have now* is a clue to find the difference between two numbers.

40. What is the answer to this problem?

    A. 160 pictures

    B. 109 pictures

    C. 218 pictures

    D. 181 pictures

SHOW YOUR WORK!

Test B | Name: _____

Directions: Read each problem carefully and select the best answer.

41. What is 761 rounded to the nearest hundred?

    A. 760

    B. 700

    C. 600

    D. 800

> Look at the number to the right of the hundreds place. Is that number 5 or greater?

42. Round 303 to the nearest ten.

    A. 310

    B. 300

    C. 303

    D. 350

43. Which number shows 1,987 rounded to the nearest hundred?

    A. 1,900

    B. 2,000

    C. 1,980

    D. 1,990

> If you round 987 to the nearest hundred, it becomes 1,000. There is already one thousand in the original number, 1,987.

44. Which number, when rounded to the tens place, is 50?

    A. 56

    B. 42

    C. 51

    D. 44

Test B   Name: _____

Directions: Read each problem carefully and select the best answer.

45. Estimate the sum by rounding each number to the nearest ten.

     A. 730

     B. 690

     $$627 + 99$$

     C. 700

     D. 720

> Be careful! Look closely at the tens places before rounding.

46. Round to the nearest hundred to estimate the sum.

     A. 1,500

     B. 1,506

     $$1,285 + 321$$

     C. 1,300

     D. 1,600

47. Leon used rounding to the nearest hundred to estimate 160 + 220 and got 300. Is his estimate correct?

     A. Yes. The number 160 rounds to 100 and the number 220 rounds to 200, so you get 300.

     B. No. The number 160 rounds to 200 and the number 220 rounds to 200, so you get 400.

     C. Yes. The number 160 rounds to 200 and the number 220 rounds to 100, so you get 300.

     D. No. The number 160 rounds to 200 and the number 220 rounds to 300, so you get 500.

> Round the numbers *before* you add them.

48. Which addition problem has a sum of about 400 when rounded to the nearest hundred?

     A. 175 + 250

     B. 325 + 275

     C. 225 + 175

     D. 250 + 275

| Test B | Name: _____ |

Directions: Read each problem carefully and select the best answer.

49. Which multiplication problem has a product of about 300?

    A. 65 x 5

    B. 35 x 9

    C. 56 x 5

    D. 44 x 5

50. Estimate the product by rounding the second factor to the nearest ten.

    A. 420

    B. 468

    C. 400

    D. 480

6 x 78

> Round the greatest factor to the nearest ten before multiplying.

51. Which two products, when rounded to the nearest ten, are the same?

    A. 55 x 5 and 61 x 5

    B. 43 x 5 and 33 x 5

    C. 24 x 6 and 34 x 3

    D. 34 x 5 and 42 x 3

> Remember, the factors can be rounded up or down depending on the digit to the right of the tens place.

52. Estimate the product by rounding the first factor to the nearest ten.

    A. 400

    B. 450

    C. 435

    D. 550

87 x 5

Test B   Name: _____

Directions: Read each problem carefully and select the best answer.

53. What fraction does the number line show?

    A. $\frac{3}{7}$

    B. $\frac{4}{7}$

    C. $\frac{4}{6}$

    D. $\frac{2}{3}$

> Think about it. How many segments is the number line divided into (denominator)? Now, count the number of segments between 0 and the dot (numerator).

54. What fraction of the shape is not shaded?

    A. $\frac{3}{4}$

    B. $\frac{1}{8}$

    C. $\frac{2}{4}$

    D. $\frac{1}{4}$

55. Twelve students went to the county fair. Eight of the students saw the horse race. What fraction of the students saw the horse race?

    A. $\frac{4}{12}$

    B. $\frac{3}{12}$

    C. $\frac{8}{12}$

    D. $\frac{6}{12}$

56. Sandy made a pizza with 8 equal slices. She put pepperoni on 5 slices. What fraction of the pizza did not have pepperoni?

    A. $\frac{3}{8}$

    B. $\frac{5}{8}$

    C. $\frac{1}{8}$

    D. $\frac{4}{8}$

> Go back and reread the problem. Be sure that you answered the question that was actually asked.

Test B   Name: _____

Directions: Read each problem carefully and select the best answer.

57. Use the fraction number lines to help you answer the question.
Which fraction is the least?

A. $\frac{4}{8}$

B. $\frac{4}{6}$

C. $\frac{1}{4}$

D. None. They are all equal.

> Circle the dot on each fraction number line before answering the question.

58. Which two fractions are equivalent?

A. $\frac{2}{3}$ and $\frac{1}{4}$

B. $\frac{1}{2}$ and $\frac{2}{3}$

C. $\frac{2}{3}$ and $\frac{3}{6}$

D. $\frac{3}{6}$ and $\frac{1}{2}$

> Use process of elimination. Which models have the same amount of shaded space?

59. What are equivalent fractions?

A. Equivalent fractions have different values, but the same denominator.

B. Equivalent fractions have different values, but the same numerator.

C. Equivalent fractions have the same value, but look different.

D. Equivalent fractions have different values and look different.

60. What is the missing number that makes these fractions equivalent?

A. 1

B. 3

C. 2

D. 4

$$\frac{6}{8} = \frac{\square}{4}$$

Test B   Name: _____

Directions: Read the word problem carefully and select the best answer.

61. Which fraction equals 1?

     A. $\frac{9}{1}$

     B. $\frac{9}{2}$

     C. $\frac{1}{9}$

     D. $\frac{9}{9}$

> Remember that fractions represent division.

62. Four friends went out for pizza. Lisa ate $\frac{3}{8}$ of her pizza, Sandy ate $\frac{4}{4}$ of her pizza, Helen ate $\frac{1}{4}$ of her pizza, and Wanda ate $\frac{5}{6}$ of her pizza. Who ate a whole pizza?

     A. Lisa

     B. Sandy

     C. Helen

     D. Wanda

> A fraction with the same numerator and denominator equals one whole.

63. Which two values would appear at the same point on a number line?

     A. $\frac{9}{1}$ and 1

     B. $\frac{9}{9}$ and 1

     C. $\frac{1}{9}$ and 1

     D. $\frac{9}{9}$ and 9

64. Express 1 as a fraction.

     A. $\frac{1}{2}$

     B. $\frac{2}{1}$

     C. $\frac{1}{12}$

     D. $\frac{2}{2}$

Test B | Name: _____

Directions: Read each problem carefully and select the best answer.

65. Which is the best estimate for the capacity of a small kitchen sink?

  A. 25L

  B. 6L

  C. 1,000 mL

  D. 600 mL

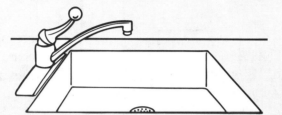

> 1 L (liter) is slightly larger than a quart.

66. Which is the best estimate for the weight of an apple?

  A. 150 kg

  B. 5 g

  C. 2 kg

  D. 150 g

67. Which is the best unit to use to measure the capacity of a coffee cup?

  A. g

  B. L

  C. mL

  D. kg

> L (liter) and mL (milliliter) measure capacity.

68. Betsy has 18 books on her bookshelf. Each book weighs 2 kilograms. How much do all of the books on the shelf weigh?

  A. 36 kilograms

  B. 16 kilograms

  C. 36 grams

  D. 9 kilograms

Test B   Name: _____

Directions: Read each problem carefully and select the best answer.

69. Which shape is not a rectangle?

A.   B.    C.   D.

> Use what you know about rectangles. A rectangle is a parallelogram with four right angles.

70. What two shapes were made by dividing the pentagon?

A. rhombus and triangle

B. triangle and parallelogram

C. triangle and rectangle

D. trapezoid and triangle

71. A polygon has two sides that are parallel. What is the least number of sides this polygon could have?

A. two

B. three

C. four

D. five

> Draw two parallel lines. How many lines do you need to add to make a closed shape?

72. This is an equilateral triangle. What is another name for this triangle?

A. obtuse triangle

B. right triangle

C. acute triangle

D. scalene triangle

Test B   Name: _____

Directions: Read each problem carefully and select the best answer.

73. Frank went to bed at the time shown on the clock.
What time did Frank go to bed?

   A. quarter to 7

   B. 9:38

   C. 8:45

   D. seven forty-five

74. Andy said it was two thirty. Eddie said it was half
past two. Who was right?

   A. Andy was right.

   B. Eddie was right.

   C. Andy and Eddie were both right.

   D. Andy and Eddie were both wrong.

> You can say the same time
> in different ways.

75. It is quarter after twelve. How many minutes is that
after 12:00?

   A. 15 minutes

   B. 45 minutes

   C. 12 minutes

   D. 30 minutes

> Count by fives from one
> number to the next to find
> how many minutes after
> the hour.

76. The minute hand is missing on this clock.
Where would the hand be placed to show 10:45?

   A. The minute hand points to 10.

   B. The minute hand points to 3.

   C. The minute hand points to 9.

   D. The minute hand is between 9
and 10.

Test B   Name: _____

Directions: Read each problem carefully and select the best answer.

77. What are two ways to say the time shown on the clock?

   A. twenty-one minutes after eight and 8:21

   B. twenty-one minutes to eight and 7:21

   C. four forty and twenty minutes to five

   D. 8:20 and twenty minutes after eight

78. What time is not shown on the clock?

   A. three thirty-nine

   B. twenty-one minutes to four

   C. twenty-one minutes to three

   D. 3:39

79. Debbie left for a party at 12:13. Which clock shows that time?

   A.   **B.**   **C.**   **D.**

Point to the minute hand. Remember, the minute hand is longer than the hour hand.

80. What is another way to say *twenty minutes to five*?

   A. five twenty

   B. twenty minutes after five

   C. 5:40

   D. 4:40

Draw a clock that shows twenty minutes to five. Think of other ways to say that time.

Test B   Name: _____

Directions: Read each problem carefully and select the best answer.

81. Ellen watched her two favorite television shows. One show was one hour long, and the other show was a half hour long. She finished watching TV at 9:30. What time did she start watching television?

    A. 9:00

    B. 8:00

    C. 8:30

    D. 11:00

82. Mrs. Leon's third grade class went on a field trip to an aquarium. The class arrived at the aquarium at 10:10 a.m. They left to go back to school at 2:30 p.m. How long did they stay at the aquarium?

    A. 4 hours

    B. 12 hours and 40 minutes

    C. 8 hours and 20 minutes

    D. 4 hours and 20 minutes

    > Draw a clock. Start at 10:10. Find the hours by moving forward until you get to 2:10. Now add the minutes until you get to 2:30.

83. Joshua was busy making a science project for school. He started working on the project at 5:25 p.m. and stopped working at 7:40 p.m. How long did Joshua work on his science project?

    A. 2 hours

    B. 1 hour and 15 minutes

    C. 2 hours and 15 minutes

    D. 2 hours and 40 minutes

84. Mary Ann went shopping at the time shown on the clock. She shopped for three hours and fifteen minutes. What time did Mary Ann finish shopping?

    A. 4:40

    B. 10:25

    C. 4:55

    D. 1:55

    > What time is shown on the clock? Start at the time shown and move forward three hours. Then move the minute hand fifteen minutes.

Test B | Name: _____

Directions: Read each problem carefully and select the best answer.

85. The horse show was in town for 6 days. How many hours was the horse show in town?

 A. 24 hours

 B. 144 hours

 C. 72 hours

 D. 360 hours

SHOW YOUR WORK!

1 day = 24 hours
Multiply the number of days the horse show was in town by 24 hours.

86. Susan was at the zoo for 4 hours and 40 minutes. How many minutes was Susan at the zoo?

 A. 240 minutes

 B. 40 minutes

 C. 100 minutes

 D. 280 minutes

SHOW YOUR WORK!

87. Jeremy took roller-skating lessons for 8 weeks and 5 days. How many days did Jeremy take skating lessons in all?

 A. 13 days

 B. 61 days

 C. 56 days

 D. 5 days

SHOW YOUR WORK!

88. Kate and her mother were planting a garden in the backyard. In the morning, they worked on the garden for 125 minutes. That afternoon, they worked for 1 hour and 40 minutes. Did Kate and her mother work longer planting the garden in the morning or the afternoon?

 A. Kate and her mother worked 25 minutes longer in the afternoon.

 B. Kate and her mother worked 15 minutes longer in the morning.

 C. Kate and her mother worked 25 minutes longer in the morning.

 D. Kate and her mother worked the same amount of time in the morning as they did in the afternoon.

Change hours into minutes, and then add 40. Now compare the times.

| Test B | Name: _____ |

Directions: Read each problem carefully and select the best answer.

89. What is the perimeter of the rectangle?

A. 18 yd.

B. 36 yd.

C. 72 yd.

D. 30 yd.

12 yd.

6 yd.

Opposite sides of a rectangle are equal lengths, so two lengths are 12 yd. and two widths are 6 yd.

90. What is the perimeter of this polygon?

A. 24 in.

B. 26 ft.

C. 28 in.

D. 26 in.

2 in.

3 in.

7 in.

8 in.

6 in.

SHOW YOUR WORK!

91. Tiffany's garden is the shape of a pentagon. Three sides are 5 meters long. The other two sides are 4 meters long. What is the perimeter of Tiffany's garden?

A. 15 meters

B. 9 meters

C. 23 meters

D. 19 meters

SHOW YOUR WORK!

92. Which rectangle has a perimeter of 30 feet?

A. length: 8 feet; width: 6 feet

B. length: 6 feet; width: 5 feet

C. length: 9 feet; width: 6 feet

D. length: 10 feet; width: 3 feet

Draw each rectangle and label the sides with the given lengths and widths. Find each perimeter.

Test B | Name: _____

Directions: Read each problem carefully and select the best answer.

93. What is the area of the figure when ☐ = 1 square unit?

- **A.** 16 units
- **B.** 14 units
- **C.** 16 square units
- **D.** 14 square units

> Two triangles equal *one* square.

94. What is the area of a rectangle with length of 12 inches and width of 9 inches?

- **A.** 48 sq. in.
- **B.** 42 sq. in.
- **C.** 108 sq. in.
- **D.** 21 sq. in.

SHOW YOUR WORK!

95. What is the area of this polygon?

- **A.** 24 sq. cm
- **B.** 22 sq. cm
- **C.** 48 sq. cm
- **D.** 11 sq. cm

3 cm

8 cm   8 cm

3 cm

SHOW YOUR WORK!

96. What is the area of the figure?

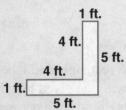

1 ft.

4 ft.

5 ft.

4 ft.

1 ft.

5 ft.

> Divide the figure into two rectangles. Find the area of each rectangle, then add the areas together.

SHOW YOUR WORK!

- **A.** 10 sq. ft.
- **B.** 9 sq. ft.
- **C.** 20 sq. ft.
- **D.** 5 sq. ft.

Test B   Name: _____

Directions: Read each problem carefully and select the best answer.

97. Which dimensions (length and width) create the rectangle with the smallest perimeter and an area of 30 sq. in.?

SHOW YOUR WORK!

Use the formula for perimeter:

$P = (2 \times l) + (2 \times w)$

   A. 10 in. and 3 in.

   B. 30 in. and 1 in.

   C. 15 in. and 2 in.

   D. 6 in. and 5 in.

98. Which rectangle has the same area as this rectangle?

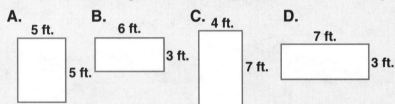

99. A rectangle has an area of 12 square centimeters. Which dimensions (length and width) are not possible for this size rectangle?

   A. 4 cm and 3 cm   **C.** 6 cm and 6 cm

   B. 12 cm and 1 cm   **D.** 6 cm and 2 cm

A rectangle cannot have an area of 12 sq. cm unless $l \times w = 12$ sq. cm

100. Which rectangle has the same perimeter *and* area?

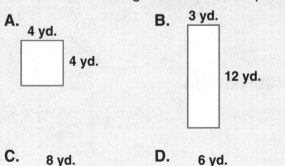

SHOW YOUR WORK!

Test C | Name: _____

Directions: Read the word problem carefully. Select the best answer for each question.

On Friday, 653 people went to a play. On Saturday, there were 848 people at the play. How many people went to the play in all?

1. What fact do you need to know to solve the problem?

   A. 653 people and 848 people went to a play.

   B. There was a play on Friday and Saturday.

   C. 653 is less than 848.

   D. 848 people went to a play.

2. What operation should you use when you see the clue phrase *in all*?

   A. multiplication

   B. addition

   C. subtraction

   D. division

3. What number sentence can be used to solve the problem?

   A. $653 + 884 = n$

   B. $848 - 653 = n$

   C. $653 \times 848 = n$

   D. $848 + 653 = n$

4. What is the answer to the word problem?

   A. 195 people

   B. 1,401 people

   C. 1,501 people

   D. 1,491 people

SHOW YOUR WORK!

Test C　　Name: _____

Directions: Look at the bar graph carefully. Select the best answer for each question.

Brandon's family was planning a vacation, but they didn't know where to go. They decided to ask their friends about their favorite vacation states. Then they tallied the information and put the data on the bar graph below.

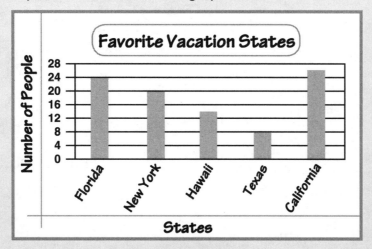

5. Do you think Brandon's family will go to Texas?

   A. Yes, because 8 people wanted to go there.

   B. No, because it was the least popular state.

   C. No, because Texas is far away.

   D. Yes, because Texas has a lot of horses.

6. Fewer people liked New York than Florida. How many fewer people liked New York?

   A. 4 people　　**C.** 22 people

   B. 20 people　　**D.** 44 people

SHOW YOUR WORK!

7. Which state had the greatest number of votes?

   A. Florida　　**C.** California

   B. New York　　**D.** Maine

8. How many people in all were asked about their favorite vacation states?

   A. 42 people　　**C.** 72 people

   B. 92 people　　**D.** 84 people

SHOW YOUR WORK!

Test C | Name: _____

Directions: Look at the pictograph carefully. Select the best answer for each question.

Students were asked to vote for their favorite colors. The pictograph below was made to show the results of those votes.

Key: ☺ = 10 Votes

Favorite Color

Colors	Number of Votes
Red	☺ ☺ ☺ ☺
Blue	☺ ☺ ☺ ☺ ☺ ☺
Yellow	☺ ☺ ☺
Green	☺ ☺ ☺

9. Which color received double the number of votes that yellow received?

   A. blue

   B. red

   C. green

   D. none

   SHOW YOUR WORK!

10. Which two colors received a total of 70 votes?

    A. red and blue

    B. yellow and red

    C. yellow and green

    D. green and red

    SHOW YOUR WORK!

11. How many more students liked blue than red?

    A. 2 students

    B. 10 students

    C. 100 students

    D. 20 students

    SHOW YOUR WORK!

12. If green received 30 more votes, how many votes would it have all together?

    A. 55 votes

    B. 3 votes

    C. 50 votes

    D. 5.5 votes

    SHOW YOUR WORK!

Test C   Name: _____

Directions: Read the word problem carefully. Select the best answer for each question.

Samantha has been saving her loose change for several weeks. She has 2 rolls of nickels. One roll of nickels holds 40 coins. Each nickel is worth 5 cents. How many coins does Samantha have all together?

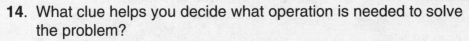

13. What fact will help you solve this word problem?
    A. Samantha has been saving change.
    B. Each nickel is worth 5 cents.
    C. Samantha has been saving for several weeks.
    D. One roll of nickels holds 40 coins.

14. What clue helps you decide what operation is needed to solve the problem?
    A. Samantha has 2 rolls of nickels.
    B. Each roll has 40 coins.
    C. all together
    D. Each nickel is worth 5 cents.

15. What operation will you use to solve the word problem?
    A. subtraction
    B. multiplication
    C. division
    D. none of the above

16. What is the answer to the word problem?
    A. $4.00
    B. 80 coins
    C. 42 coins
    D. $2.00

    SHOW YOUR WORK!

Test C   Name: _____

Directions: Read the word problem carefully. Select the best answer for each question.

Nick collects bike magazines. He has 42 magazines. Each magazine cost $2.95. He puts them in 6 equal stacks on the shelf. How many magazines are in each stack?

17. What information is not needed to solve the problem?

    A. Each magazine costs $2.95.

    B. Nick puts the magazines in 6 stacks.

    C. Nick has 42 magazines.

    D. Each stack is equal.

18. Which clue words or phrase helps you choose the operation needed to solve the problem?

    A. Each magazine cost $2.95.

    B. He puts them in equal stacks.

    C. He has 42 magazines.

    D. Nick collects bike magazines.

19. What operation will you use to solve the word problem?

    A. addition

    B. division

    C. multiplication

    D. subtraction

20. What is the answer to the word problem?

    A. 252 magazines

    B. 36 magazines

    C. 48 magazines

    D. 7 magazines

SHOW YOUR WORK!

Test C   Name: _____

Directions: Read each problem carefully and select the best answer.

21. Which fact does not belong in the same fact family as $6 \times 9 = 54$?

    A. $6 + 9 = 15$

    B. $9 \times 6 = 54$

    C. $54 \div 6 = 9$

    D. $54 \div 9 = 6$

22. What is the value of n in these related facts?

    A. 5

    B. 20

    C. 10

    D. 3

    $$5 \times n = 15$$
    $$15 \div 5 = n$$

23. Which multiplication fact is related to $48 \div 6 = 8$?

    A. $6 \times 8 = 48$

    B. $48 \div 8 = 6$

    C. $6 + 8 = 14$

    D. $8 \times 8 = 64$

24. Why aren't the given facts in the same fact family?

    $$2 \times 8 = 16$$
    $$4 \times 4 = 16$$

    A. Both facts equal 16.

    B. Both facts are multiplication.

    C. The numbers in the facts are different.

    D. All the numbers in the facts are even.

Test C | Name: _____

Directions: Read the word problems carefully. Select the best answer for each question.

At the orchard, Bob picked 96 apples. He put an equal number of apples into 6 baskets. How many apples were in each basket?

25. What does the number 96 represent?
    A. 96 stands for the number of apples in each basket.
    B. The number 96 tells how many apples were on the tree.
    C. 96 is the total number of baskets that Bob had.
    D. 96 stands for the total number of apples that Bob picked.

26. What is the answer to the word problem?
    A. $96 \div 6 = 16$ apples
    B. $96 - 6 = 90$ baskets
    C. $96 + 6 = 102$ apples
    D. $96 \div 6 = 16$ baskets

Estelle had 5 boxes of seashells. Each box had a different type of seashell. She had 8 shells in each box. How many seashells did Estelle have all together?

27. Which equation could be used to solve the problem?
    A. $8 - 5 = n$
    B. $5 + 8 = n$
    C. $5 \times 8 = n$
    D. $8 + 5 = n$

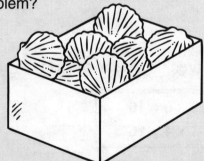

28. What is the answer to the word problem?
    A. 13 seashells
    B. 40 seashells
    C. 3 seashells
    D. 45 seashells

SHOW YOUR WORK!

Test C   Name: _____

Directions: Read each word problem carefully and select the best answer.

29. Wanda has 75 books. She decides to give away 15 outdated books and then buys 5 new books. How many books does she have?

    A. 90 books

    B. 60 books

    C. 80 books

    D. 65 books

    SHOW YOUR WORK!

30. Wanda arranges her books on her new 5-shelf bookcase. She has 60 books. If she puts an equal number of books on each shelf, how many books are on each shelf?

    A. 60 + 5 = 65   **C.** 60 x 5 = 300

    B. 60 − 5 = 55   **D.** 60 ÷ 5 = 12

    SHOW YOUR WORK!

31. Mary bought 3 tickets for the arcade for $15 each. How much money did Mary spend on arcade tickets?

    A. $18

    B. $12

    C. $5

    D. $45

    SHOW YOUR WORK!

32. In addition to buying 3 arcade tickets at $15 each, Mary bought a large soda for $1.75. How much money did Mary spend all together?

    A. $16.75   **C.** $13.25

    B. $46.75   **D.** $5.25

    SHOW YOUR WORK!

Test C   Name: _____

Directions: Read the word problem carefully. Select the best answer for each question.

Tiffany picked 51 flowers from her garden. She gave her grandmother 15 flowers. How many flowers does Tiffany still have? Tiffany equally put the rest of the flowers into 4 vases. How many flowers were in each vase?

33. What information do you need to answer the first question?

    A. Tiffany picked 51 flowers and gave her grandmother 15 flowers.

    B. Tiffany put the flowers into 4 vases.

    C. Tiffany picked 51 flowers and put them into 4 vases.

    D. Tiffany gave her grandmother 15 flowers.

34. What is the answer to the first question?

    A. 66 flowers

    B. 11 flowers

    C. 36 flowers

    D. 70 flowers

SHOW YOUR WORK!

35. What operation would you use to answer the second question?

    A. addition

    B. division

    C. subtraction

    D. multiplication

36. What is the answer to the second question?

    A. 36 flowers

    B. 9 flowers

    C. 12 flowers

    D. 8 flowers

SHOW YOUR WORK!

Test C   Name: _____

Directions: Read the multiple-step problem carefully. Select the best answer for each question.

Devin bought 3 packages of pencils for $2.37 each, a pack of markers for $9.75, and a backpack for $12.38. How much did Devin spend in all?

37. What is the hidden question in this problem?

    A. How many markers did Devin buy in all?

    B. What is the difference in price between the pencils and the markers?

    C. How much money did Devin bring with him to spend?

    D. How much did Devin spend all together for the 3 packages of pencils?

38. What equation could be used to answer the hidden question?

    A. $2.37 + 3 = n$

    B. $2.37 \times 3 = n$

    C. $9.75 + 2.37 = n$

    D. $2.37 \times 2 = n$

39. After answering the hidden question, what operation would you use to find how much Devin spent in all?

    A. addition

    B. multiplication

    C. division

    D. subtraction

40. How much did Devin spend in all?

    A. $24.50

    B. $7.11

    C. $29.24

    D. $28.24

SHOW YOUR WORK!

Test C

Name: _____

Directions: Read each problem carefully and select the best answer.

41. Which number shows 665 rounded to the nearest ten?

    A. 680

    B. 660

    C. 700

    D. 670

42. What is 989 rounded to the nearest ten?

    A. 999

    B. 980

    C. 990

    D. none of the above

43. Which number, when rounded to the nearest ten, is 540?

    A. 545

    B. 565

    C. 532

    D. 541

44. Round 999 to the nearest hundred.

    A. 900

    B. 2,000

    C. 1,000

    D. 1,009

Test C   Name: _____

Directions: Read each problem carefully and select the best answer.

45. When estimating the sum of 456 + 392, what is the greatest place the numbers could be rounded to?

    A. tens

    B. hundreds

    C. ones

    D. thousands

46. Estimate the sum by rounding each addend to the nearest ten.

    79 + 49

    A. 130

    B. 120

    C. 110

    D. none of the above

47. Estimate the sum.

    675 + 357

    A. 110

    B. 1,000

    C. 1,100

    D. 900

48. Which addition problem has a sum of about 500?

    A. 225 + 175

    B. 330 + 212

    C. 395 + 195

    D. 401 + 190

    SHOW YOUR WORK!

Test C　Name: _____

Directions: Read the word problems carefully and select the best answer.

49. Estimate the product by rounding the first factor to the nearest ten.

> **34 x 6**

A. 180
B. 240
C. 204
D. 210

SHOW YOUR WORK!

50. Estimate the product by rounding the second factor to the nearest ten.

> **8 x 64**

A. 560　　**C**. 420
B. 480　　**D**. 512

SHOW YOUR WORK!

51. The math teacher bought 9 boxes of pencils. Each box contained 64 pencils. Estimate to the nearest ten the number of pencils the teacher bought.

A. 540 pencils
B. 630 pencils
C. 585 pencils
D. 576 pencils

SHOW YOUR WORK!

52. Which multiplication problem has an estimated product of about 360?

A. 59 x 5
B. 61 x 6
C. 55 x 5
D. 69 x 6

SHOW YOUR WORK!

Test C   Name: _____

Directions: Read each problem carefully and select the best answer.

53. What fraction does the number line show?

A. $\frac{5}{10}$

B. $\frac{5}{9}$

C. $\frac{9}{5}$

D. $\frac{4}{9}$

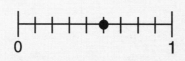

0   1

54. What fraction of the shape is shaded?

A. $\frac{1}{8}$

B. $\frac{8}{7}$

C. $\frac{7}{8}$

D. $\frac{5}{6}$

55. Rob placed 6 pencils on the desk. Two pencils roll off the desk. What fraction of pencils remain on the desk?

A. $\frac{2}{6}$

B. $\frac{6}{2}$

C. $\frac{6}{4}$

D. $\frac{4}{6}$

56. Sandy is planning an ice-cream party. She buys 2 cartons of vanilla ice cream, 1 carton of strawberry ice cream, and 2 cartons of chocolate ice cream. What fraction of the ice cream is chocolate?

A. $\frac{5}{2}$

B. $\frac{3}{5}$

C. $\frac{2}{5}$

D. $\frac{1}{5}$

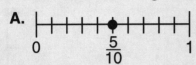

Directions: Read each problem carefully and select the best answer.

57. Which fraction is the greatest?

A.
```
|++++++•++++|
0         5        1
          10
```

B.
```
|++•++++|
0    3       1
     6
```

C.
```
|+++•+++|
0     4       1
      8
```

D. All three fractions have equal values.

58. Which list shows the fractions from least to greatest?

A. $\frac{2}{8}, \frac{2}{6}, \frac{2}{5}, \frac{2}{3}$

B. $\frac{2}{3}, \frac{2}{6}, \frac{2}{5}, \frac{2}{8}$

C. $\frac{2}{6}, \frac{2}{5}, \frac{2}{8}, \frac{2}{3}$

D. $\frac{2}{3}, \frac{2}{8}, \frac{2}{6}, \frac{2}{5}$

59. Simplify the fraction $\frac{3}{6}$.

A. $\frac{2}{3}$

B. $\frac{1}{6}$

C. $\frac{1}{2}$

D. $\frac{1}{3}$

SHOW YOUR WORK!

60. Which two fractions are equivalent to $\frac{1}{2}$?

A. $\frac{2}{6}$ and $\frac{1}{3}$

B. $\frac{5}{10}$ and $\frac{2}{5}$

C. $\frac{2}{4}$ and $\frac{3}{8}$

D. $\frac{3}{6}$ and $\frac{4}{8}$

SHOW YOUR WORK!

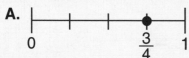

Name: _____

Directions: Read each problem carefully and select the best answer.

---

61. Which number line shows a fraction that equals 1?

A.

|——|——|——|——●——|
0           $\frac{3}{4}$ 1

B.

|—|—|—|—|—|●|—|
0            $\frac{6}{7}$ 1

C.

|—|—|—|—|●|—|
0           $\frac{5}{6}$ 1

D.

|—|—|—|—|—|—●
0            $\frac{7}{7}$

62. Express the whole number 1 as a fraction.

  A. $\frac{4}{7}$

  B. $\frac{10}{5}$

  C. $\frac{10}{10}$

  D. $\frac{5}{8}$

63. Angela finished $\frac{4}{5}$ of her homework, Crissy finished $\frac{3}{4}$ of her homework, Mike finished $\frac{1}{2}$ of his homework, and Jose finished $\frac{4}{4}$ of his homework.

Which student finished all of the homework?

  A. Angie

  B. Crissy

  C. Mike

  D. Jose

64. Which fraction is equivalent to 2?

  A. $\frac{2}{2}$

  B. $\frac{10}{5}$

  C. $\frac{1}{2}$

  D. 2

Test C   Name: _____

Directions: Read each problem carefully and select the best answer.

65. Which is the best estimate for the capacity of a spoon?

　　A. 500 mL

　　B. 5 mL

　　C. 1 L

　　D. 5 L

66. Which is the best estimate for the weight of an adult lion?

　　A. 10 kg

　　B. 250 g

　　C. 250 kg

　　D. 2,000 g

67. Ellen did an experiment. She wanted to find out how many drops of water are in a bottle that holds 3 liters of water. Each drop of water is 1 milliliter. How many drops of water were in the bottle?

　　A. 1,000 drops of water

　　B. 300 drops of water

　　C. 30,000 drops of water

　　D. 3,000 drops of water

SHOW YOUR WORK!

68. Which is the best unit to use to measure the weight of a nickel?

　　A. kg

　　B. L

　　C. g

　　D. mL

Test C   Name: _____

Directions: Read each problem carefully and select the best answer.

69. Which statement is not true about an obtuse triangle?

    A. An obtuse triangle has three obtuse angles.

    B. An obtuse triangle has two acute angles.

    C. An obtuse triangle must have one obtuse angle.

    D. An obtuse triangle can be a scalene triangle.

70. What is the name of a rectangle with four equal-length sides and four right angles?

    A. trapezoid

    B. square

    C. pentagon

    D. equilateral triangle

71. Dyana said these two shapes were quadrilaterals. Was she correct?

    A. Dyana is not correct because the first shape has right angles and the second shape does not have right angles.

    B. Dyana is not correct because the first shape is a square and the second shape is a rhombus.

    C. Dyana is correct because the shapes are the same size.

    D. Dyana is correct because both shapes have four sides.

72. Which shape is a polygon?

    A.   **B.**   **C.**   **D.**

Test C   Name: _____

Directions: Read each problem carefully and select the best answer.

73. Bob must be at school at half past 7. Which clock shows the time that Bob must be at school?

   A.   **C.**

   B.   **D.**

74. What two ways can you say the time shown on this clock?

   A. 45 minutes after 1 and quarter to 1

   B. quarter to 1 and 15 minutes to 2

   C. 15 minutes to 1 and 1:45

   D. quarter to 2 and 45 minutes after 1

75. Which answer does not represent the time on the clock?

   A. 15 minutes after 9

   B. 45 minutes after 3

   C. quarter after 9

   D. nine fifteen

76. Cam had a soccer game at half past 10. He arrived at the field at quarter after 10. Was Cam early or late for his game?

   A. Cam was 30 minutes late for his game.

   B. Cam was 45 minutes early for his game.

   C. Cam was 15 minutes late for his game.

   D. Cam was 15 minutes early for his game.

Test C   Name: _____

Directions: Read each problem carefully and select the best answer.

77. Phillip said the time was 11:35. Ronnie said it was 35 minutes to 12. Who was right?

    A. Phillip and Ronnie were both right.

    B. Phillip was right.

    C. Ronnie was right.

    D. Phillip and Ronnie were both wrong.

78. What time is shown on the clock?

    A. eighteen minutes after two

    B. eighteen minutes to two

    C. twelve minutes after four

    D. four minutes after two

79. Angelina's art class starts at 3:40. She arrived at the class at 10 minutes to 4. Was Angelina early or late for her art class?

    A. Angelina was 10 minutes early for her class.

    B. Angelina arrived exactly at 3:40.

    C. Angelina was 10 minutes late for her class.

    D. Angelina was 50 minutes late for her class.

80. Susan went to a movie that lasted 2 hours and 23 minutes. How many minutes long was the movie?

    A. 83 minutes

    B. 143 minutes

    C. 120 minutes

    D. 23 minutes

Test C	Name: _____

Directions: Read each problem carefully and select the best answer.

81. The football game started at 11:45 a.m. It ended 2 hours and 30 minutes later. What time was the game over?

   A. 2:15 a.m.

   B. 2:00 p.m.

   C. 2:15 p.m.

   D. 1:45 a.m.

SHOW YOUR WORK!

82. Kimberly arrived at the park with her friend at 1:05. It took Kimberly 10 minutes to walk from her house to her friend's house. Then it took them 15 minutes to walk to the park. What time did Kimberly leave her house?

   A. 12:40

   B. 1:30

   C. 12:55

   D. 12:50

SHOW YOUR WORK!

83. Bobby went apple picking at the time shown on the clock. He picked apples for one hour and twenty minutes. What time was Bobby finished picking apples?

   A. 4:30

   B. 4:35

   C. 4:15

   D. 3:35

SHOW YOUR WORK!

84. Jeffrey's family went to the beach. Jeffrey started playing volleyball on the beach at 10:15. He stopped playing at 12:20. How long did Jeffrey play volleyball?

   A. 2 hours

   B. 1 hour and 5 minutes

   C. 3 hours and 5 minutes

   D. 2 hours and 5 minutes

SHOW YOUR WORK!

Test C　　　Name: _____

Directions: Read each problem carefully and select the best answer.

85. The puppies were 10 weeks and 2 days old. How many days old were the puppies?

   A. 72 days

   B. 52 days

   C. 12 days

   D. 70 days

SHOW YOUR WORK!

86. Daniel was on vacation for 7 days and 1 hour. How many hours was Daniel on vacation?

   A. 8 hours

   B. 49 hours

   C. 169 hours

   D. 168 hours

SHOW YOUR WORK!

87. Bonnie painted her bedroom. It took her 3 hours and 45 minutes. How many minutes did Bonnie take to paint her bedroom?

   A. 180 minutes

   B. 165 minutes

   C. 105 minutes

   D. 225 minutes

SHOW YOUR WORK!

88. Frank had a job delivering newspapers. He worked for 6 weeks and 4 days without a day off. He told everyone that he worked 50 days without a day off. Was Frank right?

   A. Yes, Frank worked 50 days without a day off.

   B. No, Frank worked 46 days without a day off.

   C. No, Frank worked 42 days without a day off.

   D. No, Frank worked 34 days without a day off.

SHOW YOUR WORK!

Test C   Name: _____

Directions: Read each problem carefully and select the best answer.

89. Which measurements could belong to a triangle with a perimeter of 27 units?

    A. each side is 27 units long

    B. sides with lengths of 6 units, 6 units, 5 units, and 10 units

    C. each side is 9 units long

    D. sides with lengths of 7 units, 9 units, and 10 units

    SHOW YOUR WORK!

90. Which rectangle does not have the same perimeter as a rectangle with a length of 6 in. and a width of 2 in.?

    A. length: 4 in.; width: 4 in.

    B. length: 8 in.; width: 1 in.

    C. length: 7 in.; width: 1 in.

    D. length: 5 in.; width: 3 in.

    SHOW YOUR WORK!

91. What is the perimeter of the figure?

    A. 17 cm

    B. 19 in.

    C. 18 cm

    D. 19 cm

    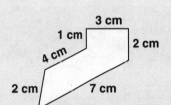

    SHOW YOUR WORK!

92. The backyard of a house is shaped like a trapezoid. Two sides are each 15 meters long. The other two sides are 11 meters and 32 meters. What is the perimeter of the backyard?

    A. 43 meters   **C.** 58 meters

    B. 30 meters   **D.** 73 meters

    SHOW YOUR WORK!

| Test C | Name: _____ |

Directions: Read each problem carefully and select the best answer.

93. Which two figures have the same area?　　☐ = 1 square unit

A. 1 and 2

B. 2 and 3

C. 1 and 3

D. none

1. 　　2. 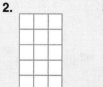　　3.

94. What is the area of the square?

5 m

SHOW YOUR WORK!

A. 25 sq. m

B. 10 sq. m

C. 5 sq. m

D. 20 sq. m

95. Blake's bedroom is 13 ft. long and 8 ft. wide. What is the area of Blake's bedroom?

A. 64 sq. ft.

B. 104 sq. ft.

C. 21 sq. ft.

D. 42 sq. ft.

SHOW YOUR WORK!

96. What is the area of the figure?

A. 36 sq. in.

B. 32 sq. in.

C. 100 sq. in.

D. 44 sq. in.

10 in.

2 in.

6 in.

8 in.

6 in.

4 in.

SHOW YOUR WORK!

Test C   Name: _____

Directions: Read each problem carefully and select the best answer.

97. Which figure has the same perimeter as a rectangle with a length of 6 m and a width of 7 m?

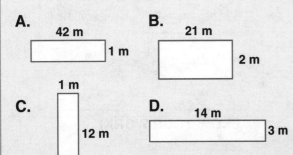

A.
42 m
1 m

B.
21 m
2 m

C.
1 m
12 m

D.
14 m
3 m

SHOW YOUR WORK!

98. Mrs. White wants to tile her bathroom floor with square tiles that are one foot in length. A diagram of the room that Mrs. White wants to tile is shown below. What are the area and the perimeter of the room?

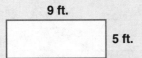

9 ft.
5 ft.

A. area: 45 sq. ft.; perimeter: 28 sq. ft.

B. area: 14 sq. ft.; perimeter: 28 ft.

C. area: 45 sq. ft.; perimeter: 28 ft.

D. area: 28 sq. ft.; perimeter: 45 ft.

SHOW YOUR WORK!

99. Which dimensions (length and width) create the rectangle with the greatest perimeter and an area of 24 sq. in.?

A. length: 6 in.; width: 4 in.

B. length: 12 in.; width: 2 in.

C. length: 8 in.; width: 3 in.

D. length: 24 in.; width: 1 in.

SHOW YOUR WORK!

100. A rectangle has an area of 36 sq. cm. Which dimensions (length and width) are not possible for this rectangle?

A. length: 9 cm; width: 4 cm

B. length: 30 cm; width: 6 cm

C. length: 12 cm; width: 3 cm

D. length: 6 cm; width: 6 cm

SHOW YOUR WORK!

Master Answer Sheet

Answers for Test A (pages 10–34)

1. C	11. B	21. B	31. D	41. D	51. C	61. B	71. A	81. C	91. B
2. B	12. A	22. A	32. B	42. B	52. B	62. C	72. D	82. B	92. D
3. C	13. B	23. C	33. A	43. C	53. C	63. C	73. C	83. D	93. B
4. D	14. C	24. C	34. B	44. D	54. D	64. D	74. A	84. A	94. D
5. C	15. C	25. B	35. B	45. C	55. C	65. C	75. A	85. D	95. C
6. D	16. D	26. D	36. D	46. D	56. B	66. D	76. B	86. C	96. A
7. B	17. D	27. C	37. C	47. C	57. B	67. A	77. B	87. A	97. C
8. A	18. C	28. D	38. A	48. B	58. A	68. C	78. C	88. B	98. B
9. C	19. D	29. C	39. D	49. B	59. D	69. B	79. D	89. D	99. A
10. C	20. C	30. D	40. C	50. C	60. A	70. C	80. A	90. A	100. C

Answers for Test B (pages 35–59)

1. D	11. D	21. C	31. D	41. D	51. A	61. D	71. C	81. B	91. C
2. B	12. C	22. D	32. D	42. B	52. B	62. B	72. C	82. D	92. C
3. A	13. D	23. D	33. C	43. B	53. B	63. B	73. D	83. C	93. D
4. B	14. B	24. A	34. B	44. C	54. D	64. D	74. C	84. C	94. C
5. C	15. D	25. C	35. C	45. A	55. C	65. B	75. A	85. B	95. A
6. D	16. C	26. C	36. D	46. D	56. A	66. D	76. C	86. D	96. B
7. D	17. D	27. B	37. B	47. B	57. C	67. C	77. A	87. B	97. D
8. D	18. D	28. A	38. C	48. C	58. D	68. A	78. C	88. C	98. B
9. B	19. B	29. B	39. D	49. C	59. C	69. B	79. B	89. B	99. C
10. A	20. B	30. C	40. A	50. D	60. B	70. D	80. D	90. D	100. A

Answers for Test C (pages 60–84)

1. A	11. D	21. A	31. D	41. D	51. A	61. D	71. D	81. C	91. D
2. B	12. A	22. D	32. B	42. C	52. B	62. C	72. A	82. A	92. D
3. D	13. D	23. A	33. A	43. D	53. B	63. D	73. A	83. B	93. B
4. C	14. C	24. C	34. C	44. C	54. C	64. B	74. D	84. D	94. A
5. B	15. B	25. D	35. B	45. B	55. D	65. B	75. B	85. A	95. B
6. A	16. B	26. A	36. B	46. A	56. C	66. C	76. D	86. C	96. D
7. C	17. A	27. C	37. D	47. C	57. D	67. D	77. B	87. D	97. C
8. B	18. B	28. B	38. B	48. B	58. A	68. C	78. A	88. B	98. C
9. A	19. B	29. D	39. A	49. A	59. C	69. A	79. C	89. C	99. D
10. B	20. D	30. D	40. C	50. B	60. D	70. B	80. B	90. B	100. B

Explanations for Test A Answers

Addition and Subtraction (page 10)

1. Correct Answer: C
Sarah is bringing in 6 blue markers is a fact that is needed to solve the problem (24 − 6 = 18).
Incorrect Answers:
A. *Sarah is doing a project* does not provide any important information needed to solve the problem; it is extraneous information.
B. *Sarah needs markers* does not tell how many markers are needed to do the project.
D. *The class will be coloring the sky* does not provide any important information needed to solve the problem; it is extraneous information.

2. Correct Answer: B
How many more is a clue that indicates that you should subtract.
Incorrect Answers:
A. *How many* is not the entire clue.
C. *Need to color* is not a clue to help you decide what operation to use.
D. *Bring in 24 markers* is not a clue about the operation; it is a number fact. *24* tells how many markers are needed in all for the project.

3. Correct Answer: C
Subtraction is the operation to use to solve the problem. *How many more* is a clue that indicates that you should subtract.
Incorrect Answers:
A. Addition is used to find a total amount, not to find how many more.
B. Multiplication is a shortcut for addition and is used to find a total amount, not to find how many more.
D. Division is used to separate an amount into equal groups and is not used to compare numbers.

4. Correct Answer: D
Begin with the 24 markers that are needed in all, and subtract the 6 markers that Sarah is bringing. That leaves 18 more markers needed (24 − 6 = 18).
Incorrect Answers:
A. 48 was calculated by adding (24 + 24 = 48).
B. 30 was calculated by adding (24 + 6 = 30), instead of subtracting (24 − 6 = 18).
C. 12 was calculated by adding 6 + 6.

Addition and Subtraction with Bar Graphs (page 11)

5. Correct Answer: C
The bar for apple is the tallest, which means it received the most votes.
Incorrect Answers:
A. B. D. These bars are shorter, and therefore they received less votes.

6. Correct Answer: D
35 people liked the plum the best.
Incorrect Answers:
A. The plum bar is higher than 30.
B. The plum bar is lower than 40.
C. 32 is not in the middle of 30 and 40. 32 is closer to 30 than to 40.

7. Correct Answer: B
The peach had 20 votes and the banana had 40 votes. 20 x 2 = 40
Incorrect Answers:
A. 45 is more than twice as many as 20.
C. 30 is less than 40.
D. 35 is less than 40.

8. Correct Answer: A
Apple received the greatest number of votes (45).
Peach received the least number of votes (20).
45 − 20 = 25
Incorrect Answers:
B. 65 is the sum of 45 and 20, not the difference.
C. 20 is the least number of votes received by a fruit, not the difference between the greatest and the least.
D. 15 is the difference between the greatest (apple) and the next-to-least (orange) number of votes. 45 − 30 = 15

Addition and Subtraction with Pictographs (page 12)

9. Correct Answer: C
There are 4 cones in the *vanilla* row, and each cone represents 2 children. 2 + 2 + 2 + 2 = 8.
Incorrect Answers:
A. Each cone represents 2 children. An answer of 4 would only represent one child per cone.
B. 2 is the number of children represented by each cone, not how many children like vanilla ice cream.
D. 5 children would be 2 ½ cones, but there are 4 cones on the pictograph for vanilla.

10. Correct Answer: C
There are 2 more cones for chocolate chip than for chocolate. Those 2 cones represent 4 more children.
Incorrect Answers:
A. 8 children chose vanilla, which is 4 less than chocolate.
B. 4 children chose strawberry, which is 8 less than chocolate.
D. 16 (chocolate chip) is 4 more than 12 (chocolate); therefore *none* is not the correct answer.

11. Correct Answer: B
Half of a cone would stand for half the amount the cone represents. 1 is half of 2. Half a cone equals 1 child.
Incorrect Answers:
A. This answer does not make sense. The cone is not real and cannot be eaten.
C. A full cone stands for 2 children.
D. If a child was not sure what flavor he liked best, his answer could not be represented on the pictograph.

12. Correct Answer: A
In all means to add.
Strawberry = 4 and chocolate = 12, and 12 + 4 = 16.
Incorrect Answers:
B. 12 is the number of children who liked chocolate ice cream. It does not include the number of children who liked strawberry ice cream.
C. 8 is the total number of cones for chocolate and strawberry. Each cone represents 2 children, so the total is 16, not 8.
D. The number of strawberry cones pictured on the graph was added to the number of chocolate chip cones on the graph. The question was about chocolate, not chocolate chip ice-cream cones.

Multiplication Within 100 (page 13)

13. Correct Answer: B
Nine groups with 3 people in each group is a fact. This fact provides the information necessary to solve the problem.
Incorrect Answers:
A. This information does not contain any facts that can be used to solve the problem.
C. This fact does not provide enough information to solve the problem.
D. This fact does not provide enough information to solve the problem.

Explanations for Test A Answers *(cont.)*

Multiplication Within 100 *(page 13)* *(cont.)*

14. Correct Answer: C
The clue words *all together* indicate that you should multiply. In this problem the number of groups (9) is multiplied by the number of people in each group (3).
- **A.** *Nine groups* is needed to solve the problem, but will not help you determine the operation.
- **B.** *How many* does not include enough information to help you determine the operation.
- **D.** *3 groups* is needed to solve the problem, but will not help you determine the operation.

15. Correct Answer: C
Multiplication is used to find the total number in equal groups. In this problem the number of groups (9) is multiplied by the number of people in each group (3).
Incorrect Answers:
- **A.** Subtraction is used to find the difference between two numbers.
- **B.** Addition could be used here, but multiplication is used as a shortcut for repeated addition.
- **D.** Division is used to split a number into equal groups.

16. Correct Answer: D
Multiply the number of groups (9) by the number of people in each group (3) to find how many people went on the trip (27).
Incorrect Answers:
- **A.** The number of groups and the number in each group were added together to incorrectly solve the problem.
- **B.** The number in each group was subtracted from the number of groups to incorrectly solve the problem.
- **C.** The number of groups was divided by the number in each group to incorrectly solve the problem.

Division Within 100 *(page 14)*

17. Correct Answer: D
This information provides the number of stickers and how many Julia wants on each page.
Incorrect Answers:
- **A.** This answer does not tell you what Julia wants to do with the stickers.
- **B.** This answer does not tell you what Julia wants to do with the stickers.
- **C.** This answer does not tell you how many stickers Julia has.

18. Correct Answer: C
Division is used to split a quantity into equal groups. In this problem, the number of stickers will be divided into equal groups.
Incorrect Answers:
- **A.** Subtraction is used to find the difference between two numbers.
- **B.** Addition is used to find the total amount of two or more numbers.
- **D.** Multiplication is used to find the total number in equal groups.

19. Correct Answer: D
This number sentence represents dividing the total number of stickers (16) into equal groups (4).
Incorrect Answers:
- **A.** Multiplication can be eliminated because it is used to find the total number in equal groups.
- **B.** Addition can be eliminated because it is used to find the total of two or more numbers.
- **C.** Subtraction can be eliminated because it is used to find the difference.

20. Correct Answer: C
To solve this problem divide the number of stickers (16) by the number of pages (4) to find out how many stickers will be on each page (4).
Incorrect Answers:
- **A.** The number of stickers (16) and the number of pages (4) were added together.
- **B.** The number of stickers (16) was multiplied by the number of pages (4).
- **D.** The number of pages (4) was subtracted from the number of stickers (16).

Relating Multiplication and Division within 100 *(page 15)*

21. Correct Answer: B
$18 \div 3 = 6$ is the related division fact. It has the same three numbers as $3 \times 6 = 18$.
Incorrect Answers:
- **A.** $18 \div 6 = 4$ is not a related fact. 4 is not one of the numbers in the fact family, and $18 \div 6$ does not equal 4.
- **C.** $6 \div 3 = 2$ is not a related fact. 2 is not one of the numbers in the fact family.
- **D.** $18 \div 6 = 6$ is not a related fact. There are not two 6s in the $3 \times 6 = 18$ fact family, and $18 \div 6$ does not equal 6.

22. Correct Answer: A
The number 8 makes both problems correct: $4 \times 8 = 32$ and $32 \div 4 = 8$.
Incorrect Answers:
- **B.** 36 was found by adding $32 + 4$. Putting 36 in the blanks does not make the equations true.
- **C.** 4×9 is not 32 ($4 \times 9 = 36$), and $32 \div 9$ is not 4.
- **D.** 4×4 is not 32 ($4 \times 4 = 16$), and $32 \div 4$ is not 4 ($32 \div 4 = 8$).

23. Correct Answer: C
$8 \times 7 = 56$ is a related fact for $56 \div 8 = 7$.
Both facts contain the same numbers, and multiplication and division are related operations.
Incorrect Answers:
- **A.** 56×8 does not equal 7.
- **B.** 15 is not one of the numbers in the fact $56 \div 8 = 7$.
- **D.** $56 - 8 = 48$ is a subtraction fact and subtraction is not related to division. Also, 48 is not one of the numbers in the fact $56 \div 8 = 7$.

24. Correct Answer: C
$7 + 5 = 12$ is not a related fact. Addition is not an operation in this fact family and 12 is not one of the numbers in $5 \times 7 = 35$.
Incorrect Answers:
- **A.** $35 \div 5 = 7$ is a related division fact for $5 \times 7 = 35$.
- **B.** $7 \times 5 = 35$ is a related multiplication fact for $5 \times 7 = 35$.
- **D.** $35 \div 7 = 5$ is a related division fact for $5 \times 7 = 35$.

Multiplication and Division Within 100 *(page 16)*

25. Correct Answer: B
Each is a clue for division.
Incorrect Answers:
- **A.** *Has 3 dogs* is a fact needed to solve the problem but it does not help you decide what operation to use to solve the problem.
- **C.** *How many* does not include enough information to help you determine the operation.
- **D.** *Bought dog treats* is not a clue. This phrase does not help you decide how to solve the problem.

Explanations for Test A Answers *(cont.)*

Multiplication and Division Within 100 *(page 16)*
(cont.)

26. Correct Answer: D
21 ÷ 3 = 7 divides the total number of treats into 3 equal groups.
Incorrect Answers:
- **A.** Multiplication does not divide the treats evenly among the dogs.
- **B.** 24 in the equation 24 ÷ 3 = 8 was calculated by adding 21 + 3. 24 was not a fact in this problem, so this cannot be the correct answer.
- **C.** Subtraction does not divide the treats evenly among the dogs.

27. Correct Answer: C
To find the total number of stickers you need to know that Willow has 4 pages and each page has 9 stickers.
Incorrect Answers:
- **A.** *9 stickers* only tells how many stickers are on each page. It is not enough information to solve the problem.
- **B.** *On each page* does not state any facts to help you solve the problem.
- **D.** *4 pages* and *9 stickers* is not enough information to solve the problem. You must know that there are 9 stickers on each of the 4 pages.

28. Correct Answer: D
4 pages x 9 stickers on each page = 36 stickers all together.
Incorrect Answers:
- **A.** 13 was calculated by adding 4 + 9. Addition is the wrong operation.
- **B.** 5 was calculated by subtracting 9 – 4. Multiplication should be used to find the total number of objects in a given number of equal groups.
- **C.** 18 was calculated by adding 9 + 9. 18 only tells how many stickers are on two pages.

Word Problems with Mixed Operations *(page 17)*

29. Correct Answer: C
Drew's pizza and soda cost $7.18 ($5.49 + $1.69).
$10.00 – $7.18 = $2.82
Incorrect Answers:
- **A.** Drew spent $7.18; this does not tell how much change he got back.
- **B.** An addition (step 1) or subtraction (step 2) error occurred.
- **D.** A subtraction (step 2) error occurred.

30. Correct Answer: D
Marco earns $8 per day ($3.00 + $5.00), and there are seven days in a week: $8.00 X 7 days per week= $56 per week.
Incorrect Answers:
- **A.** $40 is how much Marco earns in five days, but there are seven days per week.
- **B.** Marco earns $21 per week just from walking the dog; $21 does not include the money he earns from delivering newspapers.
- **C.** Marco earns $35 per week just from delivering newspapers, $35 does not include the money he earns from walking the dog.

31. Correct Answer: D
The number of cookies (6) put in each bag was multiplied by the number of bags to be filled (9) to find out how many cookies are needed (54): 6 x 9 = 54.
Incorrect Answers:
- **A.** The number of cookies in each bag was subtracted from the number of bags to be filled.
- **B.** The number of cookies in each bag was added to the number of bags to be filled.
- **C.** Possible multiplication error: 6 x 9 = 54, not 48.

32. Correct Answer: B
The total number of miles (12) was divided by the number of days (4) to determine the equal number of miles Mike jogged each day (3).
Incorrect Answers:
- **A.** The number of miles and the number of days were added together.
- **C.** The number of days was subtracted from the number of miles.
- **D.** The number of miles was mistakenly multiplied by the number of days.

Multiple-step Problems with Two Questions
(page 18)

33. Correct Answer: A
In all is a clue that indicates addition. The price of the three items that Jake bought needs to be added to find the total cost.
Incorrect Answers:
- **B.** *How much* does not provide enough information to determine which operation to use to solve.
- **C.** *Have left* is a clue that indicates subtraction; it is not relevant to answer the first question (how much Jake spent in all).
- **D.** *Gave him $45* does not indicate what operation to use to solve the problem. $45 is a fact, not a clue.

34. Correct Answer: B
Jake spent $39. Add the cost of the three items that Jake bought: $12 + $19 + $8 = $39.
Incorrect Answers:
- **A.** $31 was calculated by adding the cost of the shirt and the pants. The belt was not included.
- **C.** $20 was calculated by adding the cost of the shirt and the belt. The pants were not included.
- **D.** $84 was calculated by adding together all of the given amounts.

35. Correct Answer: B
The total cost of what Jake bought and how much money he had to spend are the two facts that are needed to solve the problem. The difference between the two numbers is the amount that Jake had left.
Incorrect Answers:
- **A.** *The cost of the pants and the cost of the shirt* does not include all of the items that Jake bought, and it does not tell how much he had to spend in all.
- **C.** *Jake had $45 to spend and he spent $20 for a shirt and a belt* does not include the price of the pants.
- **D.** *Jake still needs to buy a hat and he had $45 to spend on clothes* is not correct. The problem does not state that Jake is spending more money to buy a hat.

36. Correct Answer: D
Subtract the total cost of all the clothes that Jake bought from the total amount that Jake had to spend, and he has $6 left:
$45 - $39 = $6.
Incorrect Answers:
- **A.** $84 was calculated by adding $45 + $12 + $19 + $8 = $84. It does not show how much money Jake had left.
- **B.** $14 was calculated by first adding the cost of the shirt and the cost of the pants. That total was then subtracted from $45. The price of the belt was not included in the addition problem.
- **C.** $25 was calculated by first adding the cost of the shirt and the cost of the belt. That total was then subtracted from $45. The price of the pants was not included in the addition problem.

Explanations for Test A Answers *(cont.)*

Multiple-step Problems with a Hidden Question (page 19)

37. Correct Answer: C
How many children are in the 6 groups? is the hidden question. You will need to know how many children are in the 6 groups in order to subtract that number from 58, the total number of children.
Incorrect Answers:
A. *How many children are going to the zoo?* is not a hidden question. It is a fact stated in the word problem: 58 children are going to the zoo.
B. *What is the difference between the number of groups and the number of children in each group?* is not the hidden question. It does not make sense to find the difference in these two unrelated quantities (number of groups / number of children per group).
D. *How many children are in each group?* is not a hidden questions. It is a fact stated in the word problem: eight children are in each group.

38. Correct Answer: A
$6 \times 8 = n$ would find the answer to the hidden question. You need to know how many children in all are in these groups. The answer is subtracted from 58 to find how many children are left.
Incorrect Answers:
B. $58 - 8 = n$ will tell how many children are left if you subtract just one group of 8 children from the 58 total children.
C. Adding the number of groups to the number of children in a group will not answer the question. Also, you cannot combine children and groups. Multiplication is used to find the total number in all the groups when there are 6 groups with 8 children in each group: $6 \times 8 = 48$.
D. $8 - 6 = n$ finds the difference between two amounts. Also, you cannot subtract the number of groups from the number of children in each group. You need to find the total number of children in the 6 groups.

39. Correct Answer: D
Are left is a clue to use subtraction. Subtraction is used to find the difference between the total number of children on the trip and the total number of children that formed the 6 groups.
Incorrect Answers:
A. *In that group* is not a clue for subtraction. It tells information about the problem but does not give you a clue to determine which operation to use to solve.
B. *How many children* is not a clue for subtraction. It indicates that you are trying to find the amount in the group.
C. *How many* does not provide enough information to determine which operation to use to solve the problem.

40. Correct Answer: C
58 children in all – 48 children in the 6 groups = 10 children remaining.
Incorrect Answers:
A. The question asks how many *children*, not how many *groups*, so groups is the wrong label.
B. 48 children does not solve the problem. It is the answer to the hidden question.
D. 50 children tells how many children are left if only one group of 8 children is formed.

Estimation and Rounding (page 20)

41. Correct Answer: D
Find the tens place, which is the place you want to round. Look one place to the right, which is the ones place. The digit in the ones place (6) is greater than five, so you will round up. Replace the digit in the ones place (6) with 0 and add 1 to the tens place.
Incorrect Answers:
A. The digit in the ones place (6) increased by one (to 7) instead of the digit in the tens place.
B. The number (16) may have been incorrectly rounded down.
C. The number (16) was rounded up, but the number in the ones place (6) was not replaced with a zero.

42. Correct Answer: B
Locate the hundreds place. This is the place you want to round. Look one place to the right, which is the tens place. The digit in the tens place is greater than five, so you will round up. Replace the numbers in the ones and tens places with zeros, and add 1 to the digit in the hundreds place.
Incorrect Answers:
A. The digit in the tens place (559) is five, so the number rounds up to 600.
C. The digit in the tens place (449) is less than five, so the number rounds down to 400.
D. The number in the tens place (560) is greater than five, so the number rounds up to 600.

43. Correct Answer: C
Find the hundreds place, then look one place to the right to find the tens place. The digit in the tens place is greater than five, so you round up.
Add 1 to the digit in the hundreds place, and replace the numbers in the ones place and tens place with zeros (900).
Incorrect Answers:
A. The number was rounded to the nearest ten.
B. The number was incorrectly rounded up to the nearest ten.
D. The number was rounded down rather than up.

44. Correct Answer: D
Find the thousands place (67,345), and then look one place to the right to find the hundreds place. The digit in the hundreds place is less than five, so you will round down. The numbers in the ten thousands place and thousands place remain the same. Zeros replace the numbers in the hundreds, tens, and ones places (67,000).
Incorrect Answers:
A. The number was rounded to the nearest hundred.
B. The number was rounded to the nearest ten thousand.
C. The number was rounded up rather than down.

Estimate Sums (page 21)

45. Correct Answer: C
Round 45 to the nearest ten by looking at the digit to the right of the tens place. The digit to the right is 5 (45), so round up. Add 1 to the tens place and replace the 5 in the ones place with a 0 (50). Round 42 to the nearest ten by looking at the digit to the right of the tens place. The digit in the ones place is less than five (42), so round down. The four in the tens place remains the same, but the number 2 is replaced by a zero (40). (50 + 40 = 90)
Incorrect Answers:
A. The numbers were not rounded before adding.
B. Both numbers were rounded down. (40 + 40 = 80)
D. 85 suggests that 45 was not correctly rounded before adding. (45 + 40 = 85)

Explanations for Test A Answers *(cont.)*

Estimate Sums *(page 21)* *(cont.)*

46. Correct Answer: D
Round 35 to the nearest ten by checking the digit to the right of the tens place. The digit is a five, so round up (40). Both addends are the same, so add forty plus forty. (40 + 40 = 80)
Incorrect Answers:
- **A.** 79 rounds up to 80 because the digit to the right of the tens place is greater than five. 10 remains the same because the digit to the right of the tens place is less than five. (80 + 10 = 90)
- **B.** 69 rounds up to 70 because the digit to the right of the tens place is greater than five. 20 remains the same because the digit to the right of the tens place is less than five. (70 + 20 = 90)
- **C.** 45 and 46 both have digits greater than or equal to five in the ones places, so both numbers round up to 50. (50 + 50 = 100)

47. Correct Answer: C
Round 365 to the hundreds place. Find the hundreds place, then look one place to the right to find the tens place. The digit in the tens place is greater than five (365), so round up. Add 1 to the digit in the hundreds place, and replace the numbers in the ones place and tens place with zeros (400). Then round 545. Find the hundreds place, then look one place to the right to find the tens place. The digit in the tens place is less than five (545), so round down by leaving the digit in the hundreds place alone and replacing the numbers in the ones place and tens place with zeros (500). (400 + 500 = 900)
Incorrect Answers:
- **A.** 910 suggests that the addends were not rounded before adding. (365 + 545 = 910)
- **B.** 800 indicates that both numbers were rounded down. (300 + 500 = 800)
- **D.** 950 indicates that 365 was rounded up to the nearest hundred, and 545 was rounded to the nearest ten instead of the nearest hundred. (400 + 550 = 950)

48. Correct Answer: B
Round the number of candy bars Sandy and Helen sold to the nearest hundred. The number of candy bars Sandy sold (155) rounds up to 200. The number of candy bars Helen sold (125) rounds down 100. All together they sold about 300 candy bars.
Incorrect Answers:
- **A.** The number of candy bars that Sandy and Helen sold were rounded to the nearest ten. (160 + 130 = 290)
- **C.** The number of candy bars Sandy sold was rounded correctly to the nearest hundred (200), but the number of candy bars Helen sold was rounded to the nearest ten (130). (200 + 130 = 330)
- **D.** The number of candy bars Sandy sold was incorrectly rounded down (100). The number of candy bars Helen sold was correctly rounded down (100). (100 + 100 = 200)

Estimate Products *(page 22)*

49. Correct Answer: B
38 was rounded up to 40 then multiplied by 3; the correct estimate is 120.
Incorrect Answers:
- **A.** 38 was rounded down to 30 and then multiplied by 3.
- **C.** 114 is the exact product, not an estimate.
- **D.** 38 may have been rounded up to 40 correctly, but an error may have been made when multiplying.

50. Correct Answer: C
The second factor was rounded up to 70 and then multiplied by 4, which equals 280.
Incorrect Answers:
- **A.** 260 is the exact product, not an estimate.
- **B.** The second factor was rounded down to 60 and then multiplied by 4.
- **D.** The second factor may have been correctly rounded to 70, but then a multiplication error occurred.

51. Correct Answer: C
The first factor (45) is rounded to 50 then multiplied by 3. 50 x 3 = 150.
Incorrect Answers:
- **A.** 64 rounds down to 60. 60 x 5 = 300
- **B.** 75 rounds up to 80. 80 x 4 = 320
- **D.** 55 rounds up to 60. 60 x 2 = 120

52. Correct Answer: B
71 rounds down to 70. 70 x 6 = 420.
65 rounds up to 70.
70 x 6 = 420.
Both estimates are the same.
Incorrect Answers:
- **A.** Both 71 and 65 round to 70.
- **C.** 71 rounds down to 70, but 65 does not round down to 60. 65 will round up to 70.
- **D.** 71 does not round down to 60, and 65 does not round down to 60. Both round to 70.

Fractions *(page 23)*

53. Correct Answer: C
The number of segments between 0 and 1 is 5, which is the denominator. The number of segments between 0 and the dot is 3, which is the numerator. The fraction shown on the number line is $\frac{3}{5}$.
Incorrect Answers:
- **A.** The number of segments between 0 and 1 would be 4, and the number of segments between 0 and the dot would be 3.
- **B.** The number of segments between 0 and 1 would be 2, and the number of segments between 0 and the dot would be 1.
- **D.** The number of segments between 0 and 1 would be 6, and the number of segments between 0 and the dot would be 5.

54. Correct Answer: D
The total number of equal parts of the rectangle is 4, which is the denominator. The number of shaded parts of the rectangle is 3, which is the numerator. $\frac{3}{4}$ of the rectangle is shaded.
Incorrect Answers:
- **A.** The number of equal parts of this rectangle would be 4, and the number of shaded parts would be 1. (1 is the number of parts not shaded in the rectangle shown.)
- **B.** The number of equal parts of this rectangle would be 2, and the number of shaded parts would be 1.
- **C.** The number of equal parts of this rectangle would be 6, and the number of shaded parts would be 3.

55. Correct Answer: C
The total number of cupcakes represents the denominator (12). The number of cupcakes with sprinkles (7) represents the numerator. The fraction of cupcakes with sprinkles is $\frac{7}{12}$.
Incorrect Answers:
- **A.** $\frac{5}{12}$ represents the fraction of cupcakes that do not have sprinkles.
- **B.** $\frac{1}{7}$ indicates the facts in the problem were misinterpreted; 7 belongs in the numerator.
- **D.** $\frac{1}{12}$ represents one cupcake out of the total number of cupcakes (12).

Explanations for Test A Answers *(cont.)*

Fractions *(page 23)* *(cont.)*

56. Correct Answer: B

The total number of tomatoes Mr. Walker picked (8) represents the denominator. The number of red tomatoes he picked (3) represents the numerator. The fraction of red tomatoes is $\frac{3}{8}$.

Incorrect Answers:

A. $\frac{1}{8}$ represents one part (1 tomato) out of the total number of tomatoes (8).

C. The number of green tomatoes (5) was used for the denominator instead of the total number of tomatoes picked.

D. $\frac{5}{8}$ represents the number of green tomatoes.

Comparing Fractions *(page 24)*

57. Correct Answer: B

Look at all three number lines. The dot representing $\frac{5}{6}$ is closest to 1, and therefore is the greatest.

Incorrect Answers:

A. $\frac{3}{4}$ is equivalent to $\frac{9}{12}$. $\frac{5}{6}$ is equivalent to $\frac{10}{12}$. $\frac{9}{12} < \frac{10}{12}$, and therefore $\frac{3}{4}$ is not greater than $\frac{5}{6}$.

C. $\frac{1}{3}$ is less than $\frac{1}{2}$. Both $\frac{3}{4}$ and $\frac{5}{6}$ are greater than $\frac{1}{2}$, so $\frac{1}{3}$ is not the greatest fraction.

D. $\frac{3}{4} = \frac{9}{12}$, $\frac{5}{6} = \frac{10}{12}$, and $\frac{1}{3} = \frac{4}{12}$. $\frac{9}{12} \neq \frac{10}{12} \neq \frac{4}{12}$

58. Correct Answer: A

Use process of elimination. $\frac{1}{4}$ is less than $\frac{1}{2}$ (eliminate D). Therefore, $\frac{1}{4}$ is also less than $\frac{2}{3}$ (eliminate B). Then create equivalent fractions to compare $\frac{1}{4}$ and $\frac{2}{6}$. $\frac{1}{4} = \frac{3}{12}$; $\frac{2}{6} = \frac{4}{12}$. $\frac{3}{12}$ is less than $\frac{4}{12}$, so $\frac{1}{4}$ is less than $\frac{2}{6}$.

Incorrect Answers:

B. $\frac{2}{3}$ is greater than $\frac{1}{2}$, but $\frac{1}{4}$ is less than $\frac{1}{2}$. Therefore, $\frac{2}{3}$ is greater than $\frac{1}{4}$ and cannot be the least fraction.

C. $\frac{2}{6}$ is less than $\frac{1}{2}$ (D), but is greater than $\frac{1}{4}$ (A). Create equivalent fractions to compare $\frac{2}{6}$ and $\frac{1}{4}$. $\frac{2}{6} = \frac{4}{12}$ and $\frac{1}{4} = \frac{3}{12}$. $\frac{3}{12}$ is less than $\frac{4}{12}$, so $\frac{1}{4}$ is less than $\frac{2}{6}$. $\frac{2}{6}$ cannot be the least fraction.

D. $\frac{1}{2}$ is greater than $\frac{1}{4}$ and $\frac{2}{3}$, so it cannot be the least fraction. (Think about eating $\frac{1}{2}$ of a pizza versus $\frac{1}{4}$ of a pizza to compare mentally.)

59. Correct Answer: D

Reduce (simplify) $\frac{4}{8}$ to lowest terms: $\frac{1}{2}$. To reduce, find the greatest number that both the numerator and denominator can be evenly divided by (greatest common factor of 4 and 8). Divide the numerator and denominator by the GCF (4).

Incorrect Answers:

A. $\frac{1}{4}$ equals $\frac{2}{8}$. $\frac{2}{8}$ is less than $\frac{4}{8}$, not equal to it.

B. $\frac{1}{8}$ is less than $\frac{4}{8}$, not equal to it.

C. $\frac{1}{12}$ is less than $\frac{4}{8}$, not equal to it.

60. Correct Answer: A

Compare $\frac{1}{4}$ and $\frac{2}{8}$ by reducing $\frac{2}{8}$ to lowest terms. To reduce, find the greatest number that both the numerator and denominator can be evenly divided by (greatest common factor of 2 and 8). Divide the numerator (2) and denominator (8) by the GCF (2). $\frac{2}{8}$ is equivalent to $\frac{1}{4}$.

Incorrect Answers:

B. $\frac{1}{3}$ is greater than $\frac{1}{4}$.

C. $\frac{1}{2}$ is equal to $\frac{2}{4}$, which is greater than $\frac{1}{4}$.

D. $\frac{6}{8}$ is equal to $\frac{3}{4}$, which is greater than $\frac{1}{4}$.

More Fractions *(page 25)*

61. Correct Answer: B

$3 \div 1 = 3$

Incorrect Answers:

A. $3 \div 3 = 1$

C. $1 \div 3 \neq 3$

D. Since $3 \div 1 = 3$ (B), *none of the above* is incorrect.

62. Correct Answer: C

$6 \div 6 = 1$

Incorrect Answers:

A. $6 \div 1 = 6$

B. $1 \div 6 \neq 1$

D. $2 \div 1 = 2$

63. Correct Answer: C

$12 \div 12 = 1$

Incorrect Answers:

A. $12 \div 12 = 1$, but $1 \div 12 \neq 1$; therefore $\frac{12}{12} \neq \frac{1}{12}$

B. $12 \div 12 = 1$, but $12 \div 1 = 12$

D. $\frac{12}{12}$ is not *another way* to express $\frac{12}{12}$; they are shown in the same way.

64. Correct Answer: D

All of the fractions ($\frac{6}{6}$, $\frac{4}{4}$, $\frac{7}{7}$) appear at the same point on the number line.

Incorrect Answers:

A. All of the fractions ($\frac{6}{6}$, $\frac{4}{4}$, $\frac{7}{7}$) appear at the same point on the number line; they are all equal to 1.

B. All of the fractions ($\frac{6}{6}$, $\frac{4}{4}$, $\frac{7}{7}$) appear at the same point on the number line; they are all equal to 1.

C. All of the fractions ($\frac{6}{6}$, $\frac{4}{4}$, $\frac{7}{7}$) appear at the same point on the number line; they are all equal to 1.

Metric Units *(page 26)*

65. Correct Answer: C

14 kg is about 30 pounds, which is the weight of an average bike.

Incorrect Answers:

A. 10 g is about the weight of 10 paperclips; it is too light.

B. 2 kg is about 4 pounds; it is too light.

D. 100 g is about 3 ounces; it is too light.

66. Correct Answer: D

3 L is about 3 quarts; it is the best estimate.

Incorrect Answers:

A. 4 ml is about 4 drops of water.

B. 500 L is too much liquid for a fishbowl; it would fill about 150 fishbowls.

C. 700 mL is less than 1 liter.

67. Correct Answer: A

A liter is about a quart; it is large enough to measure the capacity of a pool.

Incorrect Answers:

B. Kilograms measure mass, not capacity.

C. A milliliter is about a drop of liquid; it is too small to measure the capacity of a pool.

D. Grams measure mass, not capacity.

Explanations for Test A Answers *(cont.)*

Metric Units *(page 26)* *(cont.)*

68. Correct Answer: C
1 business card = 1 gram. 1,000 grams = 1 kilogram,
so 1,000 business cards = 1 kilogram
and 2,000 business cards = 2 kilograms.
Incorrect Answers:
- **A.** 1,000 business cards = 1,000 g = 1 kg
- **B.** 200 business cards = 200 g
- **D.** 100 business cards = 100 g

Two-dimensional Shapes *(page 27)*

69. Correct Answer: B
A polygon is always a closed shape made with line segments.
Incorrect Answers:
- **A.** The length of the sides does not matter as long as the sides are straight and the shape is closed.
- **C.** Polygons never have curved sides. The sides must be straight.
- **D.** Two parallel sides does not mean that it is a polygon. The shape must be closed and the rest of the sides must be straight.

70. Correct Answer: C
A hexagon has 6 sides and an octagon has 8 sides: 8 − 6 = 2 fewer sides.
Incorrect Answers:
- **A.** The number of sides of a hexagon and an octagon were added instead of subtracted. *Fewer* is a clue for subtraction.
- **B.** *Eight* is the number of sides of an octagon. The number of sides of a hexagon should have been subtracted from eight to find the answer.
- **D.** *Six* is the number of sides of a hexagon. Six should have been subtracted from the number of sides of an octagon to find the answer.

71. Correct Answer: A
All the sides on a scalene triangle are different lengths. The length of at least two sides on an isosceles triangle is the same.
Incorrect Answers:
- **B.** Both triangles could have right angles.
- **C.** All the angles on a scalene triangle are different, but the angles on an isosceles triangle do not all have to be the same.
- **D.** The sides on a scalene triangle are all different lengths. An isosceles triangle has at least two sides of the same length.

72. Correct Answer: D
This shape is a pentagon. A pentagon has five sides.
Incorrect Answers:
- **A.** A quadrilateral has four sides, but this shape has five sides.
- **B.** A hexagon has six sides, but this shape has five sides.
- **C.** A triangle has three sides, but this shape has five sides.

Time to the Half Hour and Quarter Hour *(page 28)*

73. Correct Answer: C
15 minutes after and *quarter after* mean the same thing.
15 minutes is one quarter ($\frac{1}{4}$) of an hour (60 minutes).
Incorrect Answers:
- **A.** *6:15* is correct, but *15 minutes to 6* is not correct. It is not 15 minutes to 6, it is 15 minutes after 6.
- **B.** The hour and minute hands were reversed. The hour hand is on the 6, not the 3, and the minute hand is on 3, not 6.
- **D.** The hour hand is on 6, not on 3.

74. Correct Answer: A
Quarter to 9 is the same as 8:45. 8:45 is 15 minutes after 8:30, so Marie was 15 minutes late.
Incorrect Answers:
- **B.** Marie was late, but she was only 15 minutes late, not 30 minutes.
- **C.** Quarter to 9 is 8:45, which would be 15 after the start of the movie at 8:30. Therefore, Marie was 15 minutes late, not early.
- **D.** Marie got to the movie at quarter to 9, which is the same as 8:45. 45 does not indicate how many minutes she was late.

75. Correct Answer: A
Quarter to 11 means 10:45. This clock shows 11:45 or quarter to 12.
Incorrect Answers:
- **B.** 11:45 is shown on the clock. The hour hand is close to 12 and the minute hand is on 9.
- **C.** *Quarter to 12* is another way to state 11:45. When the minute hand is on 9, you can say *quarter to*.
- **D.** 15 minutes to 12 is the same as 11:45. The hour hand is close to 12 and the minute hand is on 9, which means 15 minutes until the hour of 12.

76. Correct Answer: B
One thirty is shown when the hour hand is halfway between 1 and 2 and the minute hand is on 6.
Incorrect Answers:
- **A.** The minute hand would be on 6, but the hour hand would not be on 1; it would be halfway between 1 and 2.
- **C.** The minute hand and hour hand were reversed. The hour hand would be between 1 and 2, not on the 6, and the minute hand would be on 6, not on the 1.
- **D.** The hour hand would be between 1 and 2, but the minute hand would be on 6, not between 5 and 6.

Time to the Minute *(page 29)*

77. Correct Answer: B
5:28 is shown on the clock. The hour hand is halfway between 5 and 6. The minute hand is 3 minutes past the number 5 on the clock: 25 + 3 = 28 minutes.
Incorrect Answers:
- **A.** The minute hand is not on 6; it is 2 minutes before the number 6. That means it is 28 minutes after 5, not 30 minutes.
- **C.** The hour hand would be between 6 and 7 if it were 6:28, but it is between 5 and 6, so it is 5:28.
- **D.** It is not twenty-eight minutes to 5; it is twenty-eight minutes after 5.

78. Correct Answer: C
Nineteen minutes to 7 is the same as 6:41. The hour hand is moving to the 7, and there are nineteen minutes until it is 7 o'clock.
Incorrect Answers:
- **A.** The minute hand is not exactly on the 8. It is one minute past the eight, so it is nineteen minutes to 7.
- **B.** The hour hand is moving toward the seven, not the 6, so it is 19 minutes to 7.
- **D.** It is not forty-one minutes to 6. It is forty-one minutes after 6.

79. Correct Answer: D
There are 60 minutes in an hour: 60 + 38 = 98 minutes.
Incorrect Answers:
- **A.** It was 1 hour and 38 minutes. One hour equals 60 minutes. Sixty minutes needed to be added to 38 minutes to get the total number of minutes.
- **B.** 39 minutes was calculated by adding 1 hour + 38 minutes, instead of changing the hour into 60 minutes.
- **C.** 22 minutes was calculated by subtracting 60 − 38 = 22. 60 and 38 should be added to find how many minutes in all.

Explanations for Test A Answers (cont.)

Time to the Minute (page 29) (cont.)

80. Correct Answer: A
One fifty-one is the time shown on the clock. The hour hand is almost on 2, and the minute hand is one minute past the 10.
Incorrect Answers:
  B. The hour hand is moving toward the 2; it is already past 1:00.
  C. The hour hand is still between 1 and 2; it hasn't reached 2 yet, so it is 1:51.
  D. The hour and minute hands were reversed.

Elapsed Time (page 30)

81. Correct Answer: C
3:30 to 5:30 is two hours. 5:30 to 6:00 is 30 minutes. The total time Max practiced is 2 hours and 30 minutes.
Incorrect Answers:
  A. There are two hours from 3:30 to 5:30, not one hour.
  B. Three hours would be from 3:30 to 6:30. Max's practice was only until 6:00, which is thirty minutes less than three hours.
  D. Two hours would be from 3:30 to 5:30. Max's practice was until 6:00, which is thirty minutes longer than two hours.

82. Correct Answer: B
Juan read for 25 minutes and studied for 15 minutes, which means he worked on his homework for 40 minutes 25 + 15 = 40. 40 minutes before 4:00 is 3:20 p.m.
Incorrect Answers:
  A. 4:40 p.m. was calculated by going forward on the clock 40 minutes instead of going backward 40 minutes.
  C. 3:35 p.m. was calculated by subtracting the time spent on reading (25 minutes) from 4:00. It did not include the 15 minutes that Max studied for spelling.
  D. 3:45 p.m. was calculated by subtracting the time spent on spelling (15 minutes) from 4:00. It did not include the 25 minutes that Max spent reading.

83. Correct Answer: D
Five hours after 2:00 is 7:00. 10 minutes later is 7:10.
Incorrect Answers:
  A. 7:00 is only five hours later than 2:00. Stephanie stayed 5 hours and 10 minutes.
  B. 6:10 is only four hours later than 2:00, not 5 hours.
  C. 3:10 was calculated by subtracting 2:00 from 5 hours, 10 minutes.

84. Correct Answer: A
From 8:00 p.m. to 12 a.m. is 4 hours and from 12:00 a.m. to 7 a.m. is 7 more hours: 4 + 7 = 11 hours. Add 15 more minutes to get 11 hours and 15 minutes.
Incorrect Answers:
  B. 7 hours, 15 minutes is the hour and minutes that Lily woke up, not how many hours she slept.
  C. 45 minutes was calculated by moving forward from 7:15 p.m. to 8:00 p.m. instead of moving forward on the clock from 8:00 p.m. to 7:15 a.m.
  D. 11 hours included the hours from 8:00 p.m. to 7:00 a.m. It did not include the 15 minutes Lily slept after 7:00 a.m.

Units of Time (page 31)

85. Correct Answer: D
There are 60 minutes in one hour. The Cook family drove for 5 hours: 5 hours x 60 minutes = 300 minutes.
Incorrect Answers:
  A. 12 minutes was calculated by dividing 60 minutes by 5 hours. To change hours into minutes multiply, don't divide.
  B. 150 minutes was calculated by multiplying 5 hours x 30 minutes, but there are 60 minutes in an hour. 30 minutes is a half hour.
  C. 60 minutes is the number of minutes the Cook family drove in one hour, but the family drove 5 hours.

86. Correct Answer: C
In one week there are 7 days. Charlie practiced for 4 weeks: 4 weeks x 7 days = 28 days.
Incorrect Answers:
  A. 14 days is the amount of days in 2 weeks, but Charlie practiced for 4 weeks.
  B. 20 days is 4 weeks x 5 days, but there are 7 days in a week.
  D. 7 days is the number of days in one week, but Charlie practiced for 4 weeks.

87. Correct Answer: A
3 weeks x 7 days is 21 days. Then add 3 days: 21 + 3 = 24 days.
Incorrect Answers:
  B. 21 days is the number of days in 3 weeks. It does not include the additional 3 days.
  C. 17 days is the number of days in 2 weeks, plus 3 days. Jessica went to camp for 3 weeks and 3 days, not 2 weeks and 3 days.
  D. 3 days does not include the 3 weeks that Jessica went to camp.

88. Correct Answer: B
60 minutes = 1 hour. On Monday, Carol read for 70 minutes: 60 + 10 = 70 minutes. On Wednesday, she read for 85 minutes: 85 − 70 = 15 minutes longer on Wednesday.
Incorrect Answers:
  A. Carol did not read 10 minutes longer on Monday. Carol read for 1 hour and 10 minutes (70 minutes) on Monday and 85 minutes on Wednesday. 70 minutes is not 10 minutes longer than 85 minutes.
  C. Carol read for 70 minutes on Monday and 85 minutes on Wednesday: 70 is not equal to 85.
  D. Carol did not read 15 minutes longer on Monday. Carol read for 70 minutes on Monday and 85 minutes on Wednesday. 70 minutes is not 15 minutes longer than 85 minutes.

Perimeter (page 32)

89. Correct Answer: D
All four sides were added to find the perimeter: 7 in. + 8 in. + 11 in. + 5 in. = 31 in.
Incorrect Answers:
  A. 20 in. is the total of three sides only: 7 in. + 8 in. + 5 in. All sides must be added to find the perimeter of a shape.
  B. The perimeter is 31 in. not 31 ft.
  C. 18 in. is the total of two sides only: 7 in. + 11 in. = 18 in. All sides must be added to find the perimeter of a shape.

90. Correct Answer: A
A regular polygon has all sides of equal length. A square has four equal sides, so if one side is 7 cm then the other three sides are also 7 cm. The perimeter is 28 cm: 7 cm + 7 cm + 7 cm + 7 cm = 28 cm.
Incorrect Answers:
  B. 7 cm is the length of only one side of the polygon. Perimeter is the total of all sides.
  C. 21 cm is the total of only three sides of the polygon. The polygon has four sides, therefore one side was not added.
  D. 49 cm is the area of the square found by multiplying the length times the width. Perimeter is calculated by *adding* all the sides.

91. Correct Answer: B
The soccer field is a rectangle with a length of 50 feet and a width of 25 feet: 50 ft. + 50 ft. + 25 ft. + 25 ft. = 150 ft.
Incorrect Answers:
  A. 75 ft. was calculated by adding one length of 50 ft. instead of two 50 ft. lengths and one width of 25 ft. instead of two widths of 25 ft.
  C. 100 ft. was calculated by adding the lengths and did not include the widths: 50 ft. + 50 ft. = 100 ft.
  D. 125 ft. is the total of two lengths of 50 ft. each and one width of 25 ft. One width was not included.

Explanations for Test A Answers *(cont.)*

Perimeter *(page 32) (cont.)*

92. Correct Answer: D
The square and the rectangle have perimeters of 16.
Incorrect Answers:
A. The first shape has a perimeter of 10, and the second shape has a perimeter of 12.
B. The first shape has a perimeter of 8, and the second shape has a perimeter of 12.
C. The perimeter of the first rectangle is 10. The perimeter of the second rectangle is 14.

Area *(page 33)*

93. Correct Answer: B
Each square is one sq. un.
The total number of square units is 20.
Incorrect Answers:
A. 14 sq. un. is the number of squares that border the figure. It does not include the inside squares.
C. 16 sq. un. does not include all the squares.
D. 18 sq. un. was calculated by adding all the sides, which is the perimeter of the figure. Area is found by multiplying length x width.

94. Correct Answer: D
Area is length x width: 8 ft. x 4 ft. = 32 sq. ft.
Incorrect Answers:
A. 24 sq. ft. was calculated by adding all the sides, which would be the perimeter of the figure.
B. 12 sq. ft. was calculated by adding length and width instead of multiplying them.
C. 8 ft. is the length of one side of the rectangle.

95. Correct Answer: C
Area is found by multiplying length x width:
7 in. x 6 in. = 42 sq. in.
Incorrect Answers:
A. The number 42 is correct, but the label should be sq. in., not in.
B. 13 sq. in. was calculated by adding length + width instead of multiplying.
D. 26 in. is the perimeter of the polygon, not the area.

96. Correct Answer: A
The area of one rectangle is 6 sq. cm: 3 cm x 2 cm = 6 sq. cm.
The area of the other rectangle is 14 sq. cm:
7 cm x 2 cm = 14 sq. cm.
Add the areas together to find the total area:
6 sq. cm + 14 sq. cm = 20 sq. cm.
Incorrect Answers:
B. 24 sq. cm is the perimeter of the figure. All the sides were added.
C. 35 sq. cm was calculated by multiplying the two longest sides: 7 cm x 5 cm = 35 sq. cm.
To find area, divide the figure into two shapes. Find the area of each shape, and then add them together.
D. 14 sq. cm is the area for one part of the figure. It does not include the entire figure.

Perimeter and Area *(page 34)*

97. Correct Answer: C
$(A = l \times w)$ The area of a rectangle with length of 6 ft. and width of 4 ft. = 24 sq. ft. Rectangle C also has an area of 24 sq. ft.:
8 ft. x 3 ft. = 24 sq. ft.
Incorrect Answers:
A. Rectangle A has an area of 15 sq. ft.: 5 ft. x 3 ft. = 15 sq. ft.
B. Rectangle B has an area of 10 sq. ft.: 5 ft. x 2 ft. = 10 sq. ft.
D. Rectangle D has an area of 14 sq. ft.: 7 ft. x 2 ft. = 14 sq. ft.

98. Correct Answer: B
$(A = l \times w)$ 8 cm x 2 cm = 16 sq. cm
Incorrect Answers:
A. 7 cm x 5 cm = 35 sq. cm
C. 6 cm x 3 cm = 18 sq. cm
D. 5 cm x 4 cm = 20 sq. cm

99. Correct Answer: A
A rectangle with length 32 ft. and width 1 ft. has an area of 32 sq. ft.:
32 ft. x 1 ft. = 32 sq. ft. This rectangle would have a perimeter of 66 ft.:
(32 ft. x 2) + (1 ft. x 2) = 66 ft.
Incorrect Answers:
B. A 8 ft. x 4 ft. rectangle has an area of 32 sq. ft. and perimeter of 24 ft.:
(8 ft. x 2) + (4 ft. x 2) = 24 ft. 24 ft. is not the greatest perimeter.
C. A 16 ft. x 2 ft. rectangle has an area of 32 sq. ft. and perimeter of 36 ft.:
(16 ft. x 2) + (2 ft. x 2) = 36 ft. 36 ft. is not the greatest perimeter.
D. A 6 ft. x 5 ft. rectangle has an area of 30 sq. ft., not an area of 32 sq. ft.

100. Correct Answer: C
A rectangle with a length of 7 yd. and a width of 4 yd. has a perimeter of 22 yd.:
(7 yd. x 2) + (4 yd. x 2) = 22 yd.
A rectangle with a length of 9 yd. and a width of 2 yd. also has a perimeter of 22 yd.:
(9 yd. x 2) + (2 yd. x 2) = 22 yd.
Incorrect Answers
A. P = (6 yd. x 2) + (3 yd. x 2) = 18 yd.
B. P = (8 yd. x 2) + (2 yd. x 2) = 20 yd.
D. The area is 28 sq. yd., which is equal to the area of the rectangle in the problem. However, the perimeter of the rectangle is not the same: (28 yd. x 2) + (1 yd. x 2) = 58 yd.

Explanations for Test B Answers

Addition and Subtraction *(page 35)*

1. **Correct Answer: D**
   This fact repesents the number of chocolate and vanilla cupcakes.
   Incorrect Answers:
   A. No number facts are included to solve the problem.
   B. This information is unnecessary.
   C. This information is unnecessary.

2. **Correct Answer: B**
   The clue phrase *all together* means to add.
   Incorrect Answers:
   A. Subtraction is used to find the difference between two quantities; *all together* asks you to find the total of given quantities.
   C. Multiplication is only used when you are finding the total amount of things that are in equal groups.
   D. Division is used to separate an amount into equal groups.

3. **Correct Answer: A**
   You only need to know the number of cupcakes, not what time the bakery opens.
   Incorrect Answers:
   B. This is unnecessary information.
   C. The information cannot be used to solve the problem.
   D. The answer is no, but the explanation given is irrelevant information.

4. **Correct Answer: B**
   When you add 275 plus 144, your answer is 419.
   Incorrect Answers:
   A. Errors occurred when adding in the ones and tens columns.
   C. 144 and 275 were subtracted instead of added to get the answer 131.
   D. An addition error occurred. The one was not carried into the hundreds column.

Addition and Subtraction with Bar Graphs *(page 36)*

5. **Correct Answer: C**
   The bar for hockey stops at 40 on the scale.
   Incorrect Answers:
   A. The bar for soccer is at 60.
   B. The bar for baseball is at 90.
   D. The bar for football is at 60.

6. **Correct Answer: D**
   The scale increases by 20. Starting with 0, each number increases by 20 until you get to 100.
   Incorrect Answers:
   A. The scale increases by increments of more than 10.
   B. The scale increases by increments of more than 5.
   C. 100 is the number at the top of the scale and does not indicate the interval that the scale increases between each number.

7. **Correct Answer: D**
   Football's bar is at 60 and baseball's bar is at 90.
   60 + 90 = 150
   Incorrect Answers:
   A. The wrong numbers were added.
   B. Both football and baseball were chosen by more than 30 people, so the total of the two together must be greater than 30. 60 and 90 were subreacted instead of added.
   C. The wrong numbers were added.

8. **Correct Answer: D**
   60 = soccer 40 = hockey; 60-40 = 20
   Incorrect Answers:
   A. Soccer = 60, Basketball = 70
   B. Hockey + Basketball = 40 + 70 = 110; Football = 60,
   C. 90 people chose baseball. Only 60 chose football.

Addition and Subtraction with Pictographs *(page 37)*

9. **Correct Answer: B**
   Friday and Sunday had the same number of cars. 3 cars are shown in the pictograph for each day meaning that 12 cars were washed each day. 4 + 4 + 4 = 12 or 3 x 4 = 12
   Incorrect Answers:
   A. 10 cars were washed on Thursday; 12 cars were washed on Friday.
   C. 10 cars were washed on Thursday; 12 cars were washed on Sunday.
   D. Friday and Sunday did have the same number of cars, so none is not a correct choice.

10. **Correct Answer: A**
    Saturday has $4\frac{1}{2}$ cars on the pictograph, and that equals 18 cars washed. $4 + 4 + 4 + 4 + 2 = 18$
    Incorrect Answers:
    B. Each car on the pictograph represents 4 cars washed, not 1.
    C. Saturday has $4\frac{1}{2}$ cars on the pictograph, not 5 cars.
    D. Saturday has $4\frac{1}{2}$ cars on the pictograph, not 4 cars.

11. **Correct Answer: D**
    Saturday had the greatest number of cars washed (18), and Thursday had the least (10). 18 – 10 = 8.
    Incorrect Answers:
    A. The greatest and least numbers of car symbols were subtracted ($4\frac{1}{2}$ and $2\frac{1}{2}$), but each 🚗 represents 4 cars washed.
    B. 18 and 10 were added instead of subtracted.
    C. The greatest and least numbers of 🚗 were added, and each 🚗 represents 4 cars washed.

12. **Correct Answer: C**
    On Thursday and Friday 22 cars were washed. On Saturday, only 18 cars were washed. 22 > 18, so the answer is false.
    Incorrect Answers:
    A. 12 cars were washed on Friday as well as on Sunday. 12 + 12 = 24, so this sentence is true.
    B. 10 cars were washed on Thursday. 10 < 12 (Friday and Sunday) and 10 < 18 (Saturday) so this sentence is true.
    D. The key shows that each 🚗 is equal to 4 cars washed, so this sentence is true.

Multiplication Within 100 *(page 38)*

13. **Correct Answer: D**
    Each batch of dough makes 12 cookies and *4 batches of cookie dough* are number facts needed to solve the problem.
    Incorrect answers:
    A. *Nicole decides to bake chocolate chip cookies* is irrelevant information.
    B. *Nicole will make 4 batches of cookies* is information needed to solve the problem, but it does not provide all the information necessary to solve it.
    C. *Each batch of cookie dough makes 12 cookies* is information needed to solve the problem, but it does not provide all the information necessary to solve it.

Explanations for Test B Answers *(cont.)*

Multiplication Within 100 *(page 38)* *(cont.)*

14. Correct Answer: B

In all is a clue that indicates that you should multiply. Use multiplication to find the total number in equal groups. In this problem the number of cookies each batch of dough will make (12) is multiplied by the number of batches (4).

Incorrect Answers:

A. *Decides to bake* does not provide any clues to help you solve the problem.

C. *Each batch* is information needed to solve the problem, but it is not a clue to help determine the operation.

D. *Make 4 batches* is information needed to solve the problem, but it is not a clue to help determine the operation.

15. Correct Answer: D

Multiplication is used to find the total number in equal groups. In this problem, multiply the number of cookies in each batch times the number of batches that Nicole will make.

Incorrect Answers:

A. Addition could be used here, but multiplication is used as a shortcut for repeated addition.

B. Subtraction is used to find the difference between two numbers.

C. Division is used to split a quantity into equal groups.

16. Correct Answer: C

Multiply the number of cookies in each batch (12) times the number of batches that Nicole makes (4): 12 x 4 = 48 cookies.

Incorrect Answers:

A. The number of batches of dough and the number of cookies per batch were added together.

B. The number of batches of cookies was subtracted from the number of cookies per batch.

D. The number of cookies was divided by the number of batches.

Division Within 100 *(page 39)*

17. Correct Answer: D

Six outs must be made in each inning, and *18 outs have been made so far* are number facts needed to solve the problem.

Incorrect Answers:

A. *Six outs must be made in each inning* is a true fact. However, *a total of 18 outs must be made in a game* is not true.

B. *Andrew went to a baseball game* is extra information that is not needed to solve the problem. *There must be 6 outs in each inning* is important, but it is not enough information to solve the problem.

C. *There are 9 innings in a baseball game* is extra information that is not needed to solve the problem. *18 outs have been made so far* is important, but it is not enough to solve the problem.

18. Correct Answer: D

In each inning indicates that the 18 outs were evenly distributed among the innings played (6 outs per inning). To find how many groups (innings) are created when the outs are evenly distributed among them, divide.

Incorrect Answers:

A. *How many* is part of the question being asked in this problem.

B. *Total of 18 outs* is a number fact needed to solve the problem.

C. *There are 3 outs* tells how many outs per inning each team must have.

19. Correct Answer: B

This symbol, ÷, represents division. Division is used to divide a quantity into equal groups. In this problem the total number of outs (18) will be divided into an equal number of innings (3).

Incorrect answers:

A. This symbol, +, represents addition. Addition is used to find the total of two or more numbers.

C. This symbol, –, represents subtraction. Subtraction is used to find the difference between two numbers.

D. This symbol, x, represents multiplication. Multiplication is used to find the total number of items in a given number of equal groups.

20. Correct Answer: B

Divide the total number of outs (18) by the number of outs in one inning (6) to solve the problem: 18 ÷ 6 = 3.

Incorrect Answers:

A. The total number of outs was multiplied by the number of outs in one inning.

C. The number of outs in one inning was subtracted from the total number of outs.

D. 9 innings is the total number of innings in a game.

Relating Multiplication and Division Within 100 *(page 40)*

21. Correct Answer: C

63 ÷ 9 = 7 and 7 x 9 = 63 complete the fact family since both facts have the same three numbers as the given facts: 7, 9, and 63.

Incorrect Answers:

A. 63 ÷ 9 = 7 is a related fact, but 9 + 7 = 16 is not. 16 is not a number in the fact family, and addition is not part of the given fact family.

B. 9 x 7 = 63 is a related fact, but 9 x 4 = 36 is not. 4 and 36 are not numbers in the given fact family.

D. 7 x 9 = 63 is related fact, but 7 x 7 = 49 is not. There are not two 7s, and 49 is not a number in the given fact family.

22. Correct Answer: D

3 x 7 = 21 and 21 ÷ 3 = 7

Incorrect Answers:

A. 63 was found by multiplying 3 and 21 together. 3 should be multiplied by *n*, though, not by 21. Replacing n with 63 does not make either equation true.

B. Replacing n with 8 does not make either equation true.

C. 18 was found by subtracting the given numbers from each other (21 – 3). Replacing *n* with 18 does not make either equation true.

23. Correct Answer: D

4 x 3 = 12 and 6 x 2 = 12 are not related facts because all the numbers in both equations are not the same.

Incorrect Answers:

A. All the numbers in the fact family must be the same. 12 was the only number that was the same in both facts.

B. Two facts in the same family can be multiplication.

C. Both facts do not have to be multiplication, division is also part of this fact family.

Explanations for Test B Answers *(cont.)*

Relating Multiplication and Division Within 100
(page 40) *(cont.)*

24. Correct Answer: A

4 x 7 = 28 would help Jonathan solve 28 ÷ 4. It is part of the same fact family, and multiplication and division are inverse operations.

Incorrect Answers:

B. 28 − 4 = 24 is not a related fact because subtraction and division are not in the same fact family.

C. 4 + 4 + 4 = 12 is not a related fact because addition and division are not in the same fact family, and 28 is not part of this fact.

D. 4 + 7 = 11 is not a related fact because addition and division are not in the same fact family, and 28 is not part of this fact.

Multiplication and Division Within 100 *(page 41)*

25. Correct Answer: C

6 + 6 + 6 + 6 + 6 + 6 + 6 + 6 = 8 x 6. Adding 6 eight times means 6 players were on 8 teams:
6 + 6 + 6 + 6 + 6 + 6 + 6 + 6 = 48.
6 x 8 means the 6 players on each team were multiplied by 8 teams, and it also equals 48.

Incorrect Answers:

A. 8 + 8 + 8 + 8 + 8 + 8 + 8 + 8 = 8 x 8. 8 x 8 means 8 players were multiplied by 8 teams. There were only 6 players on each team.

B. 8 + 6 does not equal 8 x 6. 8 + 6 = 14. It is the number of teams added to the number of players per team. It does not compute the total number of players on all the teams.

D. 8 − 6 does not equal 8 x 6. 8 − 6 is subtracting the number of players on each team from the number of teams. It does not indicate the total number of players on the 8 teams.

26. Correct Answer: C

There are 8 teams with 6 players on each team: 8 x 6 = 48 players.

Incorrect Answers:

A. 8 x 6 = 48 teams is not correct. There were 8 teams and 48 *players*.

B. 8 + 6 = 14 players is the number of teams added to the number of players on each team. You cannot add unlike things (teams and players).

D. 48 ÷ 6 = 8 players states that there are 8 players when in fact there are 8 teams. Also, 48 is not a given fact in the problem, so it could not be part of the expression used to solve.

27. Correct Answer: B

Use division to solve this problem because Richard needed to separate the 81 coins into equal groups of 9 to find out how many pages would be filled.

Incorrect Answers:

A. Do not use multiplication because it is not asking for a total number of coins.

C. Do not use addition because the coins are being divided into groups of 9.

D. Do not use subtraction because the problem is not asking for a comparison or a difference.

28. Correct Answer: A

81 coins ÷ 9 per page = 9 pages

Incorrect Answers:

B. 72 was calculated by subtracting 81 − 9. Subtraction is not the correct operation.

C. 90 was calculated by adding 81 + 9. Addition is not the correct operation.

D. 81 was the total number of coins that Richard collected. It does not show how many pages those coins would fill.

Word Problems with Mixed Operations *(page 42)*

29. Correct Answer: B

$2.25 per CD x 3 CDs = $6.75 rental fee. $10.00 − $6.75 = $3.25

Incorrect Answers:

A. $6.75 is the amount Michael owed for his CD rentals.

C. A multiplication (step 1) or subtraction (step 2) error occured.

D. A subtraction error may have occurred.

30. Correct Answer: C

The number of books rented (120) was multiplied by the cost of each rental ($2) to find out how much money was collected ($240).

Incorrect Answers:

A. The number of books rented was divided by the cost of each rental.

B. The number of book rentals was added to the cost of one book rental.

D. The cost of one book rental was subtracted from the total number of book rentals.

31. Correct Answer: D

The number of pieces of chocolate candy (24) was divided by the number of people (3 friends + Chrissy = 4 people) to find out the number of pieces of candy each person received (6).

Incorrect Answers:

A. The number of pieces of candy was added to the number of friends.

B. The number of friends was subtracted from the number of pieces of candy.

C. A division error occurred. Chrissy may not have been included in the number of people sharing the candy.

32. Correct Answer: D

Ava and Bella have 36 pieces of candy all together (12 + 24). 36 ÷ 2 = 18 pieces of candy per person.

Incorrect Answers:

A. A division error occurred.

B. Ava's 12 pieces of candy were not included in the total pieces of candy available before dividing.

C. Bella's 24 pieces of candy were not included in the total pieces of candy available before dividing.

Multiple-step Problems with Two Questions
(page 43)

33. Correct Answer: C

Multiplication is used when each group contains the same number of items. *In all* is a clue to use multiplication.

Incorrect Answers:

A. Addition is used to put together groups that contain different numbers of items. The number of meatballs on each sub was the same, so multiplication can be used as a shortcut for repeated addition.

B. Subtraction does not tell how many *in all*; it is used to compare two quantities or to find their difference.

D. Division does not tell how many *in all*; it is used to split a quantity into even groups.

34. Correct Answer: B

There were 4 people and each person put 3 meatballs on his sub: 4 x 3 = 12.

Incorrect Answers:

A. There were 4 people making subs, not 3.

C. There were 4 people using 3 meatballs on each sub, not two people.

D. 3 + 4 = 7 is adding the number of meatballs per sub to the number of subs; you cannot add unlike quantities to find a total.

Explanations for Test B Answers *(cont.)*

Multiple-step Problems with Two Questions
(page 43) *(cont.)*

35. Correct Answer: C
To solve the problem you need to know *the total number of meatballs Eddie and his 3 friends had on their subs.* You add that answer to *the number of meatballs Eddie's brother had on his sub* to find out how many meatballs were used on all the subs.
Incorrect Answers:
- **A.** *Eddie's brother put more meatballs on his sub than the other people* does not provide any number facts needed to solve this problem.
- **B.** *Eddie and 3 friends made subs* is not important in this part of the problem. This information was needed to answer the first question.
- **D.** *The total number of subs made* is not important in this part of the problem. This information was needed to answer the first question; now we need to know the total number of meatballs on all of those subs.

36. Correct Answer: D
12 meatballs + 4 meatballs = 16 meatballs
Incorrect Answers:
- **A.** The question asks for the total number of meatballs, not the total number of subs. Also, 5 subs were made, not 16.
- **B.** 13 meatballs was calculated by adding 9 meatballs + 4 meatballs. 9 represents only 3 people having subs with 3 meatballs on each sub, instead of 4 people; Eddie's sub was not included.
- **C.** 13 subs was calculated by including 9 meatballs for Eddie and his friends instead of 12. It is also incorrect because the answer would be meatballs, not subs.

Multiple-step Problems with a Hidden Question
(page 44)

37. Correct Answer: B
In order to calculate how many pictures Sandy had left after deleting 29 pictures you need to know how many pictures she took in all.
Incorrect Answers:
- **A.** *How many pictures did Sandy take on Monday, Tuesday, and Wednesday?* is not the hidden question. The number of pictures taken on Thursday was not included.
- **C.** *How many more pictures did she take on Monday than she took on Thursday?* is not the hidden question. We do not need to know the difference between these two days to solve the problem.
- **D.** *How many more pictures can Sandy take?* is not the hidden question. We don't need to know that information to calculate how many pictures she has now.

38. Correct Answer: C
The total number of pictures taken on the trip is 189:
53 + 48 + 37 + 51 = 189.
Incorrect Answers:
- **A.** 152 was calculated using the wrong number of pictures taken for Thursday. On Thursday, Sandy took 51 pictures, not 14.
- **B.** 136 does not include the number of pictures taken on Monday.
- **D.** 181 was calculated by adding 53 + 48 + 37 + 14 + 29. 14 was used as the number of pictures taken on Thursday, but it should be 51. 29 is the number of pictures that were deleted and should not be included in this equation.

39. Correct Answer: D
Have now is a clue for subtraction.
Incorrect Answers:
- **A.** Addition is not the correct operation because you need to find a difference, not a total number.
- **B.** Multiplication is not the correct operation because you need to find a difference between two amounts, not a total number.
- **C.** Division is not the correct operation because you are not dividing things into equal groups. In this problem you need to find the difference between two numbers.

40. Correct Answer: A
189 − 29 = 160
Incorrect Answers:
- **B.** 109 was calculated by subtracting 138 − 29. 138 is not the total number of pictures taken because it does not include the number of pictures taken on Thursday.
- **C.** 218 was calculated by adding 189 + 29. The words *have now* in the question are a clue for subtraction, not addition.
- **D.** 53 + 48 + 37 + 14 + 29 = 181. 14 is not the number of pictures taken on Thursday, and 29 should have been subtracted from the total number of pictures, not added to it.

Estimation and Rounding *(page 45)*

41. Correct Answer: D
First, find the digit in hundreds place (7). This is the place you want to round to.
Next, look one place to the right (tens place). Determine if that number (6) is five or greater. It is greater than five, so round up.
Replace all digits to the right of the hundreds place with zeros (700), and add 1 to the digit in the hundreds place (800).
Incorrect Answers:
- **A.** The number was rounded to the tens place.
- **B.** The number was rounded down. The hundreds place remained the same, zeros replaced the tens place and the ones place.
- **C.** A mistake may have been made when rounding the number.

42. Correct Answer: B
The digit to the right of the tens place (3) is less than five, so the number is rounded down. The three in the hundreds place and the zero in the tens place remain the same, and the three in ones place is replaced with a zero (300).
Incorrect answers:
- **A.** The number was rounded up.
- **C.** The number was not rounded up, and the digit in the ones place was not replaced by a zero. The number was not changed.
- **D.** This answer indicates that a mistake in rounding occurred. The digit in the tens place was rounded up to five.

43. Correct Answer: B
The digit to the right of the hundreds place (8) is greater than five, so round up.
Adding 1 to the 9 in the hundreds place results in regrouping, which causes the digit in the thousands place (1) to become 2. All the numbers to the right of the thousands place are replaced with zeros.
Incorrect Answers:
- **A.** The number was rounded down rather than rounded up.
- **C.** The number was incorrectly rounded down to the nearest ten.
- **D.** The number was rounded up to the nearest ten.

Explanations for Test B Answers *(cont.)*

Estimation and Rounding *(page 45) (cont.)*

44. Correct Answer: C
The digit to the right of the tens place (1) is less than five, which indicates the number should be rounded down. The digit in the tens place (5) remains the same, and the digit in the ones place (1) is replaced with a zero.
Incorrect Answers:
A. The digit in the ones place is greater than five, so 56 rounds up to 60.
B. The digit in the ones place is less than five, so 42 rounds down to 40.
D. The digit in the ones place is less than five, so 44 rounds down to 40.

Estimate Sums *(page 46)*

45. Correct Answer: A
To round 627 to the nearest ten look to the right of the tens place. The digit to the right (7) is greater than five, so round up. Add 1 to the tens place and replace the number in the ones place with 0 (630). Round 99 to the nearest ten. The digit to the right of the tens place is greater than five, so round up. Add 1 to the tens place, and replace the digit in the ones place with 0 (100). Finally, add: 630 + 100 = 730.
Incorrect Answers:
B. 627 was rounded to the nearest hundred, and 99 was incorrectly rounded down instead of up. (600 + 90 = 690)
C. 99 was correctly rounded up, but 627 was rounded to the nearest hundred instead of the nearest ten. (600 + 100 = 700)
D. 99 was correctly rounded up, but 627 was incorrectly rounded down. (620 + 100 = 720)

46. Correct Answer: D
Round 1,285 to the nearest hundred. Look to the right of the hundreds place; the digit (8) is greater than five, so round up. Add 1 to the digit in the hundreds place, and replace all the other digits to the right with zeros (1,300). Use the same procedure to round 321 to the nearest hundred (300). (1,300 + 300 = 1,600)
Incorrect Answers:
A. 321 was rounded down to 300, but 1,285 was incorrectly rounded down to 1,200. (1,200 + 300 = 1,500)
B. This answer indicates that the numbers were not rounded correctly; the numbers in the ones places were not replaced by zeros. (1,205 + 301 = 1506)
C. 321 was rounded down to 300, but 1,285 was incorrectly rounded to the nearest thousand instead of the nearest hundred. (1,000 + 300 = 1,300)

47. Correct Answer: B
Round 160 to the nearest hundred before adding. Find the hundreds place, and look to the right; the digit in the tens place is greater than five, so round up.
Add 1 to the hundreds place, and replace all the digits to the right with zeros (200). Round 220 to the nearest hundred before adding.
Look to the right of the hundreds place; the digit is less than five, so round down. The digit in the hundreds place remains the same, but all the numbers to the right of the hundreds place are replaced with zeros (200). (200 + 200 = 400)
Incorrect Answers:
A. 160 does not round down to 100. The digit to the right of the hundreds place is greater than five, so 160 should have been rounded up to 200.
C. 220 does not round down to 100; it rounds down to 200. The digit in the hundreds place should have remained the same, and the numbers to the right of the hundreds place should have been replaced with zeros.

D. 220 does not round up to 300; it rounds down to 200. Since the digit to the right of the hundreds place is less than five, the hundreds place should remain the same, and the digits to the right of the hundreds place should have been replaced with zeros.

48. Correct Answer: C
225 rounds down to 200 and 175 rounds up to 200. The digit to the right of the hundreds place in 225 is less than five, so the 2 in the hundreds place remains the same and the numbers to the right of the hundreds place are replaced with zeros.
The number to the right of the hundreds place in 175 is greater than five, so 1 is added to the hundreds place and the numbers to the right of the hundreds place are replaced with zeros. (200 + 200 = 400)
Incorrect Answers:
A. 175 rounds up to 200, and 250 rounds up to 300. 200 + 300 = 500
B. 325 rounds down to 300, and 275 rounds up to 300. 300 + 300 = 600
D. 250 rounds up to 300, and 275 rounds up to 300. 300 + 300 = 600

Estimate Products *(page 47)*

49. Correct Answer: C
The factor 56 rounds to 60: 60 x 5 = 300.
Incorrect Answers:
A. 65 rounds to 70: 70 x 5 = 350.
B. 35 rounds to 40: 40 x 9 = 360.
D. 44 rounds to 40: 40 x 5 = 200.

50. Correct Answer: D
78 rounds up to 80: 80 x 6 = 480.
Incorrect Answers:
A. 78 was rounded down to 70 and was multiplied by 6 resulting in an estimate of 420.
B. 468 is an exact answer, not an estimate.
C. 78 may have been rounded up to 80 and then a multiplication error may have occurred.

51. Correct Answer: A
The first factor in 55 x 5 rounds up to 60; 60 x 5 = 300.
The first factor in 61 x 5 rounds down to 60; 60 x 5 = 300.
Both multiplication problems have the same estimate.
Incorrect Answers:
B. 43 rounds down to 40; 40 x 5 = 200. 33 rounds down to 30; 30 x 5 = 150. The multiplication problems do not have the same estimate.
C. 24 rounds down to 20; 20 x 6 = 120. 34 rounds down to 30; 30 x 3 = 90. The multiplication problems do not have the same estimate.
D. 34 rounds down to 30; 30 x 5 = 150. 42 rounds down to 40; 40 x 3 = 120. The multiplication problems do not have the same estimate.

52. Correct Answer: B
87 rounds to 90; 90 x 5 = 450.
Incorrect Answers:
A. 87 was incorrectly rounded down to 80; 80 x 5 = 400.
C. 435 is an exact answer; it is not an estimate.
D. 87 could have been correctly rounded to 90, but then incorrectly multiplied by 5.

Explanations for Test B Answers *(cont.)*

Fractions *(page 48)*

53. Correct Answer: B
The total number of segments between 0 and 1 is 7, which is the denominator. The number of segments between 0 and the dot is 4, which is the numerator. The fraction shown on the number line is $\frac{4}{7}$.
Incorrect Answers:
A. This answer represents that the number of segments between 0 and 1 is 7, and the number of segments between 0 and the dot is 3.
C. This answer represents that number of segments between 0 and 1 is 6, and the number of segments between 0 and the dot is 4.
D. This answer represents that number of segments between 0 and 1 is 3, and the number of segments between 0 and the dot is 2.

54. Correct Answer: D
The total number of equal parts of the circle is 4, which is the denominator. The number of parts not shaded in the circle is 1, which is the numerator. $\frac{1}{4}$ of the circle is not shaded.
Incorrect Answers:
A. This fraction represents the part of the circle that is shaded.
B. This fraction represents that the total number of equal parts in the circle is 8, and the number of parts not shaded is 1.
C. This fraction represents the total number of equal parts in the circle is 4, and the number of parts not shaded is 2.

55. Correct Answer: C
The total number of students that went to the county fair (12) represents the denominator. The number of students that saw the horse race (8) represents the numerator. The fraction of students that saw the horse race is $\frac{8}{12}$.
Incorrect Answers:
A. This fraction indicates that 12 students went to the county fair, and 4 students saw the horse race.
B. This fraction indicates that 12 students went to the county fair, and 3 students saw the horse race.
D. This fraction indicates that 12 students went to the county fair, and 6 students saw the horse race.

56. Correct Answer: A
The total number of equal parts (8 slices of pizza) is the denominator. The number of slices without pepperoni is the numerator (3). The fraction of the pizza with no pepperoni is $\frac{3}{8}$.
Incorrect Answers:
B. This fraction indicates there were 8 equal slices of pizza, and 5 slices did not have pepperoni.
C. This fraction indicates there were 8 equal slices of pizza, and 1 slice did not have pepperoni.
D. This fraction indicates there were 8 equal slices of pizza and that 4 slices did not have pepperoni.

Comparing Fractions *(page 49)*

57. Correct Answer: C
Look at all three number lines. $\frac{1}{4}$ is closest to 0, so it is the least fraction.
Incorrect Answers:
A. $\frac{4}{8} = \frac{1}{2}$. $\frac{1}{4}$ (C) $< \frac{1}{2}$, so $\frac{1}{4} < \frac{4}{8}$. $\frac{4}{8}$ is not the least fraction.
B. $\frac{4}{6} > \frac{1}{2}$. $\frac{1}{4}$ (C) $< \frac{1}{2}$, so $\frac{1}{4} < \frac{4}{6}$. $\frac{4}{6}$ is not the least fraction.
D. This answer indicates that all the fractions are equivalent; they are not.

58. Correct Answer: D
The shaded area of the model representing $\frac{3}{6}$ and the shaded area of the model representing $\frac{1}{2}$ are the same. The fractions $\frac{3}{6}$ and $\frac{1}{2}$ have the same value; they are equivalent fractions.
Incorrect Answers:
A. The shaded areas of $\frac{2}{3}$ and $\frac{1}{4}$ are not the same and do not have the same value. They are not equivalent fractions.
B. The shaded areas of $\frac{1}{2}$ and $\frac{2}{3}$ are not the same and do not have the same value. They are not equivalent fractions.
C. The shaded areas of $\frac{2}{3}$ and $\frac{3}{6}$ are not the same and do not have the same value. They are not equivalent fractions.

59. Correct Answer: C
Equivalent fractions have the same value, but look different. For example, if you eat 2 pieces of a 4-slice pizza ($\frac{2}{4}$), it is the same as eating $\frac{1}{2}$ of the pizza: $\frac{2}{4} = \frac{1}{2}$.
Incorrect Answers:
A. Equivalent fractions must have different denominators.
B. Equivalent fractions have different numerators.
D. Equivalent fractions do look different, but they have the same value.

60. Correct Answer: B
Looking at the denominators, what do you need to do to 8 to get 4? Divide by 2. Divide the numerator by 2 as well ($6 \div 2$) to determine the missing numerator (3).
Incorrect Answers:
A. $\frac{1}{4} \ne \frac{6}{8}$; $\frac{1}{4} = \frac{2}{8}$
C. $\frac{2}{4} \ne \frac{6}{8}$; $\frac{2}{4} = \frac{4}{8}$
D. $\frac{4}{4} \ne \frac{6}{8}$; $\frac{4}{4} = 1$

More Fractions *(page 50)*

61. Correct Answer: D
$9 \div 9 = 1$
Incorrect Answers:
A. $9 \div 1 = 9$
B. $9 \div 2 = 4\frac{1}{2}$
C. $1 \div 9 \ne 1$

62. Correct Answer: B
Sandy ate 4 pieces out of a total of 4 pieces of pizza: $4 \div 4 = 1$.
Incorrect Answers:
A. Lisa ate 3 pieces out of a total of 8 pieces of pizza; that is not the whole pizza.
C. Helen ate 1 piece out of a total of 4 pieces of pizza; that is not the whole pizza.
D. Wanda ate 5 pieces out of a total of 6 pieces of pizza; that is not the whole pizza.

63. Correct Answer: B
$9 \div 9 = 1$
Incorrect Answers:
A. $9 \div 1 = 9$, so $\frac{9}{1} \ne 1$.
C. $1 \div 9 \ne 1$; $1 \div 9 < 1$
D. $9 \div 9 = 1$, so $\frac{9}{9} \ne 9$.

64. Correct Answer: D
$2 \div 2 = 1$.
Incorrect Answers:
A. $1 \div 2 = 0.5$, so $\frac{1}{2} \ne 1$.
B. $2 \div 1 = 2$, so $\frac{2}{1} \ne 1$.
C. $1 \div 12 \ne 1$, so $1 = 12 < 1$.

Explanations for Test B Answers *(cont.)*

Metric Units *(page 51)*

65. Correct Answer: B
1 L = about 1 quart.   A sink would have a capacity of about 6 L.
Incorrect Answers:
A. 25 L would overflow a sink.
C. 1,000 mL is 1 L. It is not enough to fill a sink.
D. 600 mL is less than 1 L. It is not enough to fill a sink.

66. Correct Answer: D
150 g is about 5 ounces; it is the best estimate.
Incorrect Answers:
A. 150 kg is about 330 pounds.
B. 5 g is about the weight of 5 paper clips. An apple weighs more.
C. 2 kg is about 4 pounds.

67. Correct Answer: C
A mL is about a drop of liquid. It would be used to measure the capacity of a coffee cup.
Incorrect Answers:
A. Grams measure mass, not capacity.
B. 1 L is about 1 quart; it is too large to measure the capacity of a coffee cup.
D. Kilograms measure mass, not capacity.

68. Correct Answer: A
18 books x 2 kilograms per book = 36 kilograms
Incorrect Answers:
B. 16 kilograms was calculated by subtracting 2 kilograms from 18 books.
C. Grams is an incorrect label.
D. 9 kilograms was calculated by dividing 18 books by 2 kilograms. Division is used to separate items into groups, not to find how much in all.

Two-dimensional Shapes *(page 52)*

69. Correct Answer: B
This parallelogram is not a rectangle. Rectangles have four right angles. This shape has two acute angles and two obtuse angles.
Incorrect Answers:
A. A square is a rectangle. A square has four right angles and the opposite sides are parallel.
C. and **D.** These shapes are rectangles. They both have four right angles and opposite sides are parallel.

70. Correct Answer: D
The pentagon is divided into a trapezoid and a triangle.
A trapezoid has four sides, and one pair of the sides is parallel.
A triangle is a polygon with three sides.
Incorrect Answers:
A. A rhombus is a parallelogram with four sides of equal length. The bottom shape does not have four equal sides, so it cannot be a rhombus.
B. The bottom shape is not a parallelogram because two of the sides are not parallel.
C. The shape on the bottom is not a rectangle. Rectangles have right angles, but this shape has two acute angles and two obtuse angles.

71. Correct Answer: C
If a polygon has two parallel sides, the least number of sides it could have would be four. It is four because parallel lines never meet, so you would have to connect the parallel lines with two more lines.
Incorrect Answers:
A. *Two* is incorrect because there are already two parallel lines, so you would have to add two more lines to connect them to form a polygon.
B. If you only used three lines, your shape would not be closed or the lines would not be parallel. A polygon is a closed shape.
D. You can complete the polygon with four sides, so five is not the least number of sides you could use to complete the shape.

72. Correct Answer: C
An acute triangle has all angles less than 90°.
Incorrect Answers:
A. An obtuse triangle has one angle that is greater than 90°, but this triangle has three acute angles.
B. A right triangle has one right angle, but this triangle has three acute angles.
D. A scalene triangle has no sides that are the same length, but this triangle has three equal sides.

Time to the Half Hour and Quarter Hour *(page 53)*

73. Correct Answer: D
Frank went to bed at seven forty-five. The hour hand is closer to 8 than to 7, and the minute hand is on 9.
Incorrect Answers:
A. The hour hand would be between 6 and 7 if the time was quarter to 7; the hour hand on this clock is between 7 and 8.
B. The hour hand and the minute hand were mixed up. The hour hand was between 7 and 8, not on 9. The minute hand was on 9, not between 7 and 8.
C. The hour hand would be between 8 and 9 if the time was 8:45; the hour hand on this clock is between 7 and 8.

74. Correct Answer: C
Two thirty and half past 2 are different ways of saying the same time, so Andy and Eddie are both right. The clock shows 2:30.
Incorrect Answers:
A. Andy was right, but Eddie was also correct; they both said *2:30* in different ways.
B. Eddie was right, but Andy was also correct; they both said *2:30* in different ways.
D. Andy and Eddie both said the time correctly, but in different ways. Neither of them was wrong.

75. Correct Answer: A
Quarter after means 15 minutes after the hour. There are 60 minutes in an hour, and 15 is $\frac{1}{4}$ (one quarter) of 60.
Incorrect Answers:
B. 45 minutes would be quarter to the hour. The minute hand would be on the 9.
C. 12 is the hour, not how many minutes it is after 12.
D. 30 minutes would be half past the hour. The minute hand would be on the 6.

76. Correct Answer: C
To show 45 minutes after the hour, the minute hand would be on 9.
Incorrect Answers:
A. The time would be 10:50 if the minute hand pointed to 10.
B. The time would be 10:15 if the minute hand pointed to 3.
D. If the minute hand is between 9 and 10 it is showing more than 45 minutes. The minute hand must be exactly on 9 to show 45 minutes after the hour.

Explanations for Test B Answers *(cont.)*

Time to the Minute *(page 54)*

77. Correct Answer: A
The hour hand is just past the 8, so it is after 8:00.
The minute hand is one minute past the 4, so it is 21 minutes after the hour (8). It is 8:21.
Incorrect Answers:
B. *Twenty-one minutes to eight* (7:39) and *7:21* are not the same time.
C. The hour hand would be between 4 and 5, and the minute hand would be on 8.
D. The hour hand would be just past the 8, but the minute hand would be on 4 exactly.

78. Correct Answer: C
Twenty-one minutes to three would be 2:39. The hour hand would be between 2 and 3 instead of between 3 and 4.
Incorrect Answers:
A. The hour hand is between 3 and 4, so it is after 3:00. The minute hand is 9 minutes past the 6, so it is 39 minutes after the hour; it is 3:39.
B. 3:39 is *twenty-one minutes to four.*
D. The hour hand is between 3 and 4, so it is after 3:00. The minute hand is 9 minutes past the 6, so it is 39 minutes after the hour; it is 3:39.

79. Correct Answer: B
The hour hand is just past 12, so it is after 12:00. The minute hand is 3 minutes past the 2, which is 13 minutes after the hour; it is 12:13.
Incorrect Answers:
A. This clock shows 3:00.
C. This clock shows 12:15.
D. This clock shows 1:13.

80. Correct Answer: D
4:40 means that 40 minutes have passed since 4:00. There are 60 minutes between 4:00 and 5:00. Since 40 minutes have passed out of 60 minutes total, there are 20 minutes remaining until 5:00.
Incorrect Answers:
A. *5:20* is 20 minutes *after* 5, not to 5.
B. *twenty minutes after 5* is 5:20 and means that 5:00 has passed; *twenty minutes to five* means that it's not yet 5:00.
C. *5:40* is 40 minutes *after* 5:00; *twenty minutes to five* means that it's not yet 5:00.

Elapsed Time *(page 55)*

81. Correct Answer: B
One hour before 9:30 would be 8:30. A half hour (or 30 minutes) before 8:30 is 8:00.
Incorrect Answers:
A. If Ellen started watching TV at 9:00, she would have only watched the half-hour-long show.
C. If Ellen started watching TV at 8:30, she would have only watched the one-hour-long show.
D. 11:00 is 1 hour and 30 minutes after 9:30, but it should be 1 hour and 30 minutes before 9:30 to show when Ellen started to watch TV.

82. Correct Answer: D
10:10 to 2:10 is 4 hours. 2:10 to 2:30 is 20 minutes. The total time the class stayed at the aquarium was 4 hours, 20 minutes.
Incorrect Answers:
A. 4 hours is the time between 10:10 and 2:10. It does not include the time between 2:10 and 2:30.
B. 12 hours and 40 minutes was calculated by adding 10:10 and 2:30.
C. 8 hours and 20 minutes was calculated by subtracting the arrival and departure times: 10 hours – 2 hours = 8 hours and 30 minutes – 10 minutes = 20 minutes.

83. Correct Answer: C
It is 2 hours from 5:25 to 7:25. It is 15 minutes from 7:25 to 7:40. Joshua worked on his project for 2 hours and 15 minutes.
Incorrect Answers:
A. Two hours is the amount of time from 5:25 to 7:25. It does not include the 15 minutes from 7:25 to 7:40.
B. It is 2 hours from 5:25 to 7:25 and then 15 more minutes from 7:25 until 7:40, so *1 hour and 15 minutes* is incorrect.
D. 5:00 may have been used as the start time.

84. Correct Answer: C
The time shown on the clock is 1:40. Three hours after 1:40 is 4:40. 15 minutes after 4:40 is 4:55.
Incorrect Answers:
A. 4:40 is 3 hours after 1:40, but Mary Ann shopped for 3 hours and 15 minutes.
B. 10:25 is 3 hours and 15 minutes before 1:40, instead of 3 hours and 15 minutes after 1:40.
D. 1:55 is 15 minutes after 1:40 instead of 3 hours and 15 minutes after 1:40.

Units of Time *(page 56)*

85. Correct Answer: B
There are 24 hours in one day.
The horse show was in town for 6 days:
6 days x 24 hours = 144 hours.
Incorrect Answers:
A. 24 hours is the number of hours in one day. The horse show was in town for 6 days.
C. 72 hours was calculated by multiplying 6 days x 12 hours, but there are 24 hours in 1 day.
D. 360 hours was calculated by multiplying 6 days x 60. 60 is the number of minutes in an hour, not the number of hours in 1 day.

86. Correct Answer: D
There are 60 minutes in 1 hour.
4 hours x 60 minutes = 240 minutes.
Then add 40 minutes: 240 + 40 = 280 minutes.
Incorrect Answers:
A. 240 minutes is the number of minutes in 4 hours. It does not include the additional 40 minutes.
B. 40 minutes does not include the number of minutes in 4 hours.
C. 100 minutes was calculated by adding 60 minutes (1 hour) to 40 minutes. Susan was at the zoo for 4 hours and 40 minutes, not 1 hour and 40 minutes.

87. Correct Answer: B
8 weeks x 7 days = 56 days. Then add 5 more days:
56 + 5 = 61 days.
Incorrect Answers:
A. 13 days was calculated by adding the number of weeks to the number of days: 8 weeks + 5 days = 13. 8 weeks should be converted into the number of days in 8 weeks (56 days).
C. 56 days is the number of days in 8 weeks; it does not include the additional 5 days Jeremy took roller-skating lessons.
D. 5 days does not include the 8 weeks Jeremy took roller-skating lessons.

Explanations for Test B Answers (cont.)

Units of Time (page 56) (cont.)

88. Correct Answer: C
In the morning Kate and her mother worked 125 minutes. In the afternoon they worked 100 minutes: one hour = 60 minutes, so 60 + 40 = 100 minutes. 125 minutes – 100 minutes = 25 minutes longer in the morning.
Incorrect Answers:
A. Kate and her mother worked 125 minutes in the morning and 100 minutes in the afternoon. 125 is 25 minutes longer than 100 minutes.
B. Kate and her mother did work longer in the morning than in the afternoon, but it was 25 minutes longer, not 15 minutes longer: 125 – 100 = 25.
D. In the morning they worked 125 minutes, and in the afternoon they worked 1 hour and 40 minutes (100 minutes): 125 > 100.

Perimeter (page 57)

89. Correct Answer: B
The rectangle has 2 sides with 12 yd. lengths and 2 sides with 6 yd. lengths: (2 x 12 yd.) + (2 x 6 yd.) = 36 yd.
Incorrect Answers:
A. 18 yd. is the sum of one length and one width. Perimeter is the sum of all four sides.
C. 72 yd. is calculated using the formula for area of a rectangle (l x w) instead of perimeter.
D. 30 yd. is the sum of two lengths and one width. It does not include all four sides.

90. Correct Answer: D
Add the lengths of all sides to find perimeter:
2 in. + 8 in. + 6 in. + 7 in. + 3 in. = 26 in.
Incorrect Answers:
A. 24 in. does not include the side that is 2 in. long.
B. *26* is correct but *ft.* is not.
C. 28 in. includes an extra side that is 2 in. long.

91. Correct Answer: C
Add all 5 sides of the pentagon to find perimeter:
5 m + 5 m + 5 m + 4 m + 4 m = 23 meters.
Incorrect Answers:
A. 15 m is the sum of 3 sides of the pentagon; it does not include the 2 sides that are 4 m long.
B. 9 m was calculated by adding one 5 meter length and one 4 meter length. 3 sides of the pentagon were not included.
D. 19 m is the sum of the 3 sides that are 5 meters long and 1 side that is 4 meters long. It does not include the fifth side that is 4 meters long.

92. Correct Answer: C
All of the sides are added to find the perimeter:
9 ft. + 9 ft. + 6 ft. + 6 ft. = 30 ft.
Incorrect Answers:
A. 8 ft. + 8 ft. + 6 ft. + 6 ft. = 28 ft.
B. 6 ft. + 6 ft. + 5 ft. + 5 ft. = 22 ft.
D. 10 ft. + 10 ft. + 3 ft. + 3 ft. = 26 ft.

Area (page 58)

93. Correct Answer: D
4 triangles equal two squares. 2 sq. un. + 12 sq. un. = 14 sq. un.
Incorrect Answers:
A. The triangles were counted as squares, and the label is incorrect.
B. The label is incorrect.
C. The triangles were counted as squares, but the label is correct.

94. Correct Answer: C
Area = *length* x *width*: 12 in. x 9 in. = 108 sq. in.
Incorrect Answers:
A. 48 sq. in. was calculated by multiplying 12 (length) x 4. 4 is the number of sides in the rectangle and is not a factor in finding its area.
B. 42 is the perimeter.
D. 21 sq. in. was calculated by adding length (12) and width (9) instead of multiplying.

95. Correct Answer: A
Area = length x width: 8 cm x 3 cm = 24 sq. cm.
Incorrect Answers:
B. 22 is the perimeter.
C. 48 sq. cm was calculated by multiplying one length by one width (8 cm x 3 cm = 24 sq. cm), multiplying the remaining length and width (8 cm x 3 cm = 24 sq. cm), and then adding the two products together (24 sq. cm + 24 sq. cm = 48 sq. cm).
To find area, multiply just one length by one width.
D. 11 sq. cm was calculated by adding one length and one width instead of multiplying.

96. Correct Answer: B
To find the area of an irregular shape, divide the figure into regular shapes, find the area of each shape, and then add them together. 1st rectangle: A = 5 ft. x 1 ft. = 5 sq. ft.
2nd rectangle: A = 4 ft. x 1 ft. = 4 sq. ft.
Total: A = 5 sq. ft. + 4 sq. ft. = 9 sq. ft.
Incorrect Answers:
A. 10 sq. ft. was calculated by adding the longest length and the longest width: 5 ft. + 5 ft.
C. 20 is the perimeter.
D. 5 sq. ft. is the area for one part of the figure; it does not include the entire figure.

Perimeter and Area (page 59)

97. Correct Answer: D
P = (2 x l) + (2 x w). P = (2 x 6) + (2 x 5) = 22 in. 22 in. is the smallest perimeter for a rectangle with an area of 30 sq. in.
Incorrect Answers:
A. P = (2 x 10) + (2 x 3) = 26 in. 26 in. > 22 in.
B. P = (2 x 30) + (2 x 1) = 62 in. 62 in. > 22 in.
C. P = (2 x 15) + (2 x 2) = 34 in. 34 in. > 22 in.

98. Correct Answer: B
A = l x w. 9 ft. x 2 ft. = 18 sq. ft. and 6 ft. x 3 ft. = 18 sq. ft.
Incorrect Answers:
A. 5 ft. x 5 ft. = 25 sq. ft.
C. 7 ft. x 4 ft. = 28 sq. ft.
D. 7 ft. x 3 ft. = 21 sq. ft.

99. Correct Answer: C
A = l x w. 6 cm x 6 cm = 36 sq. cm
Incorrect Answers:
A. 4 cm x 3 cm = 12 sq. cm
B. 12 cm x 1 cm = 12 sq. cm
D. 6 cm x 2 cm = 12 sq. cm

100. Correct Answer: A
P = (2 x l) + (2 x w) = (2 x 4 yd.) + (2 x 4 yd.) = 16 yd.
A = l x w = (4 yd. x 4 yd.) = 16 sq. yd.
Incorrect Answers:
B. P = (2 x 12 yd.) + (2 x 3 yd.) = 30 yd.;
A = (12 yd. x 3 yd.) = 36 sq. yd.
C. P = (2 x 8 yd.) + (2 x 3 yd.) = 22 yd.;
A = (8 yd. x 3 yd.) = 24 sq. yd.
D. P = (2 x 6 yd.) + (2 x 2 yd.) = 16 yd.;
A = (6 yd. x 2 yd.) = 12 sq. yd.

Explanations for Test C Answers

Addition and Subtraction (page 60)

1. Correct Answer: A
653 and 848 people are the number facts needed to find how many people went to the play in all.
Incorrect Answers:
B. This information is not necessary to solve the problem.
C. The relationship between the two numbers is irrelevant; the two numbers are being combined to find how many in all.
D. *848 people* is information needed to solve the problem, but the information is incomplete.

2. Correct Answer: B
In all means to add.
Incorrect Answers:
A. Multiplication can be used with *in all*, but only when finding the total number of items in equal groups.
C. Subtraction is used to find the difference between two numbers.
D. Division is used to split a quantity into equal groups.

3. Correct Answer: D
Add the number of people who came to the play on Friday and Saturday to find how many went to the play in all.
Incorrect Answers:
A. 884 is an error; it should be 848.
B. Subtraction is the wrong operation; *in all* is a clue to add.
C. Multiplication is the wrong operation; the number of people that went on Friday and Saturday are not equal groups.

4. Correct Answer: C
653 people on Friday + 848 people on Saturday = 1,501 people in all.
Incorrect Answers:
A. 653 was subtracted from 848; subtraction is the wrong operation.
B. Addition error: The 1 that was carried from the tens column was not added to the hundreds column.
D. Addition error: The 1 that was carried from the ones column was not added to the tens column.

Addition and Subtraction with Bar Graphs (page 61)

5. Correct Answer: B
Texas had the least number of votes for favorite vacation state.
Incorrect Answers:
A. Families would want to go to the state that had the most votes, not the least number of votes.
C. The distance between Brandon's home and Texas has nothing to do with the information on the bar graph.
D. The number of horses in Texas has nothing to do with the information on the bar graph.

6. Correct Answer: A
The clue word *fewer* means subtract: 24 – 20 = 4.
Incorrect Answers:
B. 20 only represents the number of people who chose New York; it does not represent the difference between the number of people who chose Florida and New York.
C. The wrong numbers were subtracted.
D. The wrong operation was used; 20 and 24 were added instead of subtracted.

7. Correct Answer: C
The bar for California was the tallest, which indicates the greatest number of votes.
Incorrect Answers:
A. Florida had 24 votes and California had 26 votes: 24 < 26.
B. New York had 20 votes and California had 26 votes: 20 < 26.
D. Maine was not on the graph.

8. Correct Answer: B
The clue words *in all* indicate that the amounts represented by the bars should be added: 24 + 20 + 14 + 8 + 26 = 92.
Incorrect Answers:
A. Florida's and California's votes were not included in the total.
C. New York's votes were not included in the total.
D. Texas's votes were not included the total.

Addition and Subtraction with Pictographs (page 62)

9. Correct Answer: A
Yellow received 30 votes. 30 x 2 = 60. Blue received 60 votes.
Incorrect Answers:
B. Red received 40 votes. 40 ≠ 30 x 2
C. Green received 25 votes. 25 ≠ 30 x 2
D. *None* is incorrect because blue is the correct answer.

10. Correct Answer: B
Yellow = 30, Red = 40: 30 + 40 = 70
Incorrect Answers:
A. Red = 40, Blue = 60: 40 + 60 = 100
C. Yellow = 30, Green = 25: 30 + 25 = 55
D. Green = 25, Red = 40: 25 + 40 = 65

11. Correct Answer: D
Blue = 60, Red = 40: 60 – 40 = 20
Incorrect Answers:

A. The key was used incorrectly. Each ☺ was counted as one student instead of ten students.

B. Each ☺ was counted as one student instead of ten, and then the numbers were added instead of subtracted.

C. The totals for blue and red were added instead of subtracted.

12. Correct Answer: A
25 + 30 = 55
Incorrect Answers:

B. *3* is the number of additional ☺ symbols that would be added to the pictograph to represent the additional 30 votes.

C. The ☾ was not included in the sum.

D. *5.5* is the number of ☺ symbols that would represent the new total in the pictograph.

Multiplication Within 100 (page 63)

13. Correct Answer: D
Knowing the number of coins in each roll will help you find how many coins Samantha has all together.
Incorrect Answers:
A. *Samantha has been saving change* is not a number fact; knowing this will not help you solve the problem.
B. *A nickel is worth 5 cents* is extra information and will not help you solve the problem.
C. *Samantha has been saving for several weeks* is not a number fact; knowing this will not help you solve the problem.

14. Correct Answer: C
All together is a clue that indicates that you should multiply. In this problem you will multiply the number of coins per roll times the number of rolls to solve the problem.
Incorrect Answers:
A. *Samantha has 2 rolls of nickels* is a fact that will help you solve the problem, but it does not help you determine what operation to use.
B. *Each roll has 40 coins* is a fact that will help you solve the problem, but it does not help you determine what operation to use.
D. *Each nickel is worth 5 cents* is unnecessary information.

Explanations for Test C Answers *(cont.)*

Multiplication Within 100 (page 63) *(cont.)*

15. Correct Answer: B
Multiplication is used to find the total number of items in equal groups. Multiply 40 coins per roll times 2 rolls to solve the problem.
Incorrect Answers:
A. Subtraction is used to find the difference between two numbers.
C. Division is used to split a quantity into equal groups.
D. Use multiplication (B) to solve.

16. Correct Answer: B
There are 40 coins in each roll and Samantha has 2 rolls: 40 coins per roll x 2 rolls = 80 coins.
Incorrect Answers:
A. $4.00 is the total value of the nickels.
C. The number of coins in one roll (40) was added to the number of rolls (2).
D. $2.00 is the value of one roll of nickels.

Division Within 100 (page 64)

17. Correct Answer: A
The cost of each magazine is unrelated to the number of magazines per stack.
Incorrect Answers:
B. *Nick puts the magazines in 6 stacks* is a number fact needed to determine how many magazines are in each stack.
C. *Nick has 42 magazines* is a number fact needed to determine how many magazines are in each stack.
D. *Each stack is equal* is information that is needed to determine how many magazines are in each stack.

18. Correct Answer: B
He puts them in equal stacks indicates that division is the operation needed to solve this problem. Division is used to separate an amount into equal groups.
Incorrect Answers:
A. The cost of each magazine will not help determine what operation to use to solve the problem.
C. *He has 42 magazines* will not help determine what operation to use to solve the problem.
D. *Nick collects bike magazines* is not useful information.

19. Correct Answer: B
Division is used to separate a quantity into equal groups. In this problem the total number of magazines (42) is divided into an equal number of stacks (6): 42 magazines ÷ 6 stacks = 7 magazines per stack.
Incorrect Answers:
A. Addition is used to find the total amount of two or more numbers.
C. Multiplication is repeated addition.
D. Subtraction is used to find the difference between two numbers.

20. Correct Answer: D
Divide the total number of magazines (42) by number of equal stacks (6): 42 magazines ÷ 6 stacks = 7 magazines per stack.
Incorrect Answers:
A. The total number of magazines (42) was multiplied by the number of equal stacks (6).
B. The number of equal stacks (6) was subtracted from the total number of magazines (42).
C. The number of magazines (42) was added to the number of equal stacks (6).

Relating Multiplication and Division Within 100 (page 65)

21. Correct Answer: A
15 is not a number in the given fact, and addition is not in the same fact family as multiplication.
Incorrect Answers:
B. 9 x 6 = 54 contains the same numbers as the given fact, and multiplication is part of the given fact family.
C. 54 ÷ 6 = 9 contains the same numbers as the given fact, and division is in the same fact family as multiplication.
D. 54 ÷ 9 = 6 contains the same numbers as the given fact, and division is in the same fact family as multiplication.

22. Correct Answer: D
5 x 3 = 15 and 15 ÷ 5 = 3. Both equations are true when *n* is replaced with 3.
Incorrect Answers:
A. 5 x 5 ≠15 and 15 ÷ 5 ≠ 5
B. 5 x 20 ≠15 and 15 ÷ 5 ≠ 20
C. 5 x 10 ≠15 and 15 ÷ 5 ≠ 10

23. Correct Answer: A
6 x 8 = 48 is a related multiplication fact because it contains the same numbers as 48 ÷ 6 = 8.
Incorrect Answers:
B. 48 ÷ 8 = 6 is a division fact, not a multiplication fact.
C. 6 + 8 = 14 is an addition fact, not a multiplication fact.
D. 8 x 8 = 64 is not a related fact because it does not contain the same numbers as 48 ÷ 6 = 8.

24. Correct Answer: C
All facts in a fact family contain the same three numbers.
Incorrect Answers:
A. Two facts can have the same product and still be in the same family (e.g. 2 x 8 = 16 and 8 x 2 = 16).
B. Two facts can be multiplication and still be in the same fact family.
D. Even or odd is irrelevent to belonging to the same fact family.

Multiplication and Division Within 100 (page 66)

25. Correct Answer: D
96 is the total number of apples that Bob picked.
Incorrect Answers:
A. The number of apples in each basket is unknown.
B. The problem does not state how many apples are on the tree; it states how many apples Bob picked from the tree.
C. The problem states that there are 6 baskets, not 96 baskets.

26. Correct Answer: A
Bob divided 96 apples equally into 6 baskets
96 apples ÷ 6 baskets = 16 apples per basket
Incorrect Answers:
B. The number of baskets (6) was subtracted from the total number of apples (96). Unlike quantities cannot be subtracted; you cannot take 6 *baskets* away from 96 *apples*.
C. *96 + 6 = 102 apples* is incorrect because the total number of apples (96) was added to the number of baskets (6). Unlike quantities cannot be added; 96 apples and 6 baskets does not result in 102 apples.
D. The label is incorrect. The question asks how many apples, not how many baskets.

Explanations for Test C Answers (cont.)

Multiplication and Division Within 100 (page 66) (cont.)

27. Correct Answer: C
$5 \times 8 = n$ shows that Estelle had 5 boxes with 8 seashells in each box.
Incorrect Answers:
A. $8 - 5 = n$ shows 5 boxes being taken away from the number of seashells in each box. You cannot subtract unlike quantities; 5 boxes cannot be subtracted from 8 shells.
B. $5 + 8 = n$ adds together groups that contain different items. You cannot combine 5 boxes and 8 seashells into one quantity.
D. $8 + 5 = n$ adds together groups that contain different items. You cannot combine 8 seashells and 5 boxes into one quantity.

28. Correct Answer: B
5 boxes x 8 shells per box = 40 shells
Incorrect Answers:
A. 13 was calculated by adding the 5 boxes to the 8 seashells. You cannot add unlike things (boxes and seashells).
C. 3 was calculated by subtracting the 5 boxes from 8 seashells. You cannot subtract unlike things (boxes from seashells), and subtraction does not tell how many *all together*.
D. A multiplication error occurred.

Word Problems with Mixed Operations (page 67)

29. Correct Answer: D
75 books – 15 discarded books = 60 books
60 books + 5 new books = 65 books
Incorrect Answers:
A. The number of books were all added together instead of subtracting the 15 discarded books.
B. 60 does not include the five new books purchased.
C. The 5 new books were added to Wanda's 75 books, but the 15 discarded books were not subtracted from the total.

30. Correct Answer: D
The number of books (60) is divided by the number of shelves (5) to find the equal number of books on each shelf (12).
Incorrect Answers:
A. Books (60) and shelves (5) are unlike things and cannot be added together. Also, addition does not tell how many books are on *each shelf*.
B. Books (60) and shelves (5) are unlike things and cannot be subtracted from each other. Also, subtraction does not tell how many books are on *each* shelf.
C. Multiplication tells how many books there would be in all if each shelf had 60 books.

31. Correct Answer: D
Multiply the number of arcade tickets (3) by the cost of each ticket ($15) to find the amount of money Mary spent in all on arcade tickets ($45).
Incorrect Answers:
A. The cost of one arcade ticket was added to the number of tickets purchased; tickets and dollars are unlike things and cannot be added together.
B. The number of tickets purchased was subtracted from the cost of one ticket; tickets and dollars are unlike things and cannot be subtracted from each other.
C. The cost of one ticket ($15) was divided by the number of tickets bought (3); division does not tell how much Mary spent *in all*.

32. Correct Answer: B
(3 x $15 per ticket) + $1.75 = $45 + $1.75 = $46.75
Incorrect Answers:
A. The cost of one arcade ticket was added to the cost of one large soda.
C. The cost of one large soda was subtracted from the cost of one arcade ticket.
D. The cost of one large soda was multiplied by the number of tickets bought.

Multiple-step Problems with Two Questions (page 68)

33. Correct Answer: A
You need to know that Tiffany picked 51 flowers and gave her grandmother 15 flowers. Subtract these numbers to find how many flowers Tiffany has left.
Incorrect Answers:
B. *Tiffany put the flowers into 4 vases* is not relevant to the first question; the first question does not mention vases.
C. Tiffany picked 51 flowers, but she did not put them all into vases; the first question does not mention vases.
D. *Tiffany gave her grandmother 15 flowers* is information needed to solve the problem, but it is not enough information to solve.

34. Correct Answer: C
Still have is a clue to subtract; the problem is asking for the difference between the number of flowers Tiffany picked and the number of flowers that she had left: $51 - 15 = 36$.
Incorrect Answers:
A. 66 was calculated by adding 51 flowers and 15 flowers. *Still have* is a clue for subtraction, not addition.
B. 11 was calculated by subtracting 4 vases from 15 flowers. Vases and flowers are unlike things and cannot be subtracted from each other.
D. 70 was calculated by adding all of the given numbers together: $51 + 15 + 4$. Vases and flowers are unlike things and cannot be added together. Also, *still have* is a clue for subtraction, not addition.

35. Correct Answer: B
Division is used to separate the flowers equally into 4 vases.
Incorrect Answers:
A. Addition is used to find how many items in all, not how many per group.
C. Subtraction is used to find the difference between two quantities.
D. Multiplication is used for repeated addition.

36. Correct Answer: B
36 flowers ÷ 4 vases = 9 flowers per vase
Incorrect Answers:
A. 36 was calculated by subtracting: $51 - 15$. 36 is how many flowers Tiffany had left in all, not how many per vase.
C. 12 was calculated based on 51 flowers being divided among 4 vases instead of 36 flowers.
D. A division error occurred.

Multiple-step Problems with a Hidden Question (page 69)

37. Correct Answer: D
You need to find how much Devin spent on pencils in order to find how much he spent in all.
Incorrect Answers:
A. The number of markers that Devin bought is not information used to find how much money he spent; the problem states that he spent $9.75 on markers.
B. The difference between how much Devin spent on pencils and markers is not needed to find how much he spent in all.
C. The amount of money that Devin had with him does not help find how much he actually spent.

38. Correct Answer: B
$2.37 x 3 = n is the correct equation to show the total cost for all the pencils: $2.37 x 3 = $7.11.
Incorrect Answers:
A. Dollars ($2.37) and packages (3) are unlike things and cannot be added together.

Explanations for Test C Answers *(cont.)*

Multiple-step Problems with a Hidden Question
(page 69) *(cont.)*

C. The hidden question is how much Devin spent on pencils. $9.75 is the amount he spent on markers and is not relevant to the hidden question.

D. Devin bought 3 packages of pencils, not 2.

39. Correct Answer: A
In all is a clue for addition.
Incorrect Answers:
B. Multiplication is used for repeated addition. The amounts being added to solve this problem are different (they do not repeat).
C. Division is used to separate an amount into equal groups; it will not show how much he spent *in all*.
D. Subtraction is used to find the difference between two amounts, not how much *in all*.

40. Correct Answer: C
Find the sum of all the items Devin purchased:
$7.11 + $9.75 + $12.38 = $29.24.
Incorrect Answers:
A. $24.50 was calculated by adding $2.37 + $9.75 + $12.38. $2.37 is the price for one package of pencils, not 3 packages.
B. $7.11 is the cost of all the pencils. It does not include the cost of the markers and the backpack.
D. An addition error occurred.

Estimation and Rounding *(page 70)*

41. Correct Answer: D
First, find the digit in the tens place (6). This is the place you want to round. Next, look one place to the right; the digit (5) is 5 or greater, so round up. Replace the digit to the right of the tens place with 0, and add 1 to the digit in the tens place: 670.
Incorrect Answers:
A. 2 was added to the tens place instead of 1.
B. The number was rounded down rather than up.
C. The number was rounded to the nearest hundred.

42. Correct Answer: C
The digit in the ones place (9) is greater than 5, so 1 is added to the digit in the tens place and 0 replaces the digit in the ones place: 990.
Incorrect Answers:
A. The digit in the ones place was not replaced with 0.
B. The number was rounded down rather than up.
D. Since the correct answer is C, this answer cannot be correct.

43. Correct Answer: D
The digit in the ones place (1) is less than 5, so the digit in the tens place (4) remains the same, and the digit in the ones place (1) is replaced by 0:540.
Incorrect Answers:
A. 545 rounds up to 550.
B. 565 rounds up to 570.
C. 532 rounds down to 530.

44. Correct Answer: C
The digit in the hundred place (9) rounds up to ten, and the digits to the right of the hundreds place are replaced with zeros.
Incorrect Answers:
A. 999 was incorrectly rounded down.
B. 1,000 is closer to 999 than 2,000.
D. All the numbers to the right of the hundreds place were not replaced by zeros.

Estimate Sums *(page 71)*

45. Correct Answer: B
Both numbers have three digits and neither can be rounded to a four digit number, so the hundreds place is the greatest place these numbers can be rounded.

Incorrect Answers:
A. The tens place is not the greatest place value in either number because both numbers have three digits, which is the hundreds place.
C. The ones place is not the greatest place value in either number because both numbers have three digits, which is the hundreds place.
D. Both numbers have only three digits (hundreds) and neither rounds to a four-digit number (thousands).

46. Correct Answer: A
79 rounds to 80 and 49 rounds to 50: 80 + 50 =130.
Incorrect Answers:
B. 79 was correctly rounded up to 80, but 49 was rounded down to 40: 80 + 40 = 120.
C. 79 was incorrectly rounded down to 70, and 49 was incorrectly rounded down to 40: 70 + 40 = 110.
D. The correct answer is 130 (A), and therefore *none of the above* is incorrect.

47. Correct Answer: C
675 rounds to 700, and 357 rounds to 400: 700 + 400 = 1,100.
Incorrect Answers:
A. An addition error occurred; a zero was omitted from the sum.
B. 675 was correctly rounded to 700, but 357 was incorrectly rounded down to 300: 700 + 300 = 1,000.
D. 675 was incorrectly rounded down to 600, and 375 was incorrectly rounded down to 300: 600 + 300 = 900.

48. Correct Answer: B
Round both numbers to nearest hundred and then add. Find the hundreds place and look to the right; if the digit to the right is less than five round down. 330 rounds to 300 and 212 rounds to 200: 300 + 200 = 500.
Incorrect Answers:
A. 225 rounds to 200, and 175 rounds to 200: 200 + 200 = 400.
C. 395 rounds to 400, and 195 rounds to 200: 400 + 200 = 600.
D. 401 rounds to 400, and 190 rounds to 200: 400 + 200 = 600.

Estimate Products *(page 72)*

49. Correct Answer: A
34 rounds to 30, and 30 x 6 = 180.
Incorrect Answers:
B. 34 was incorrectly rounded to 40: 40 x 6 = 240.
C. 204 is the exact answer; it is not an estimate.
D. 34 was rounded to 35 (the nearest five): 35 x 6 = 210.

50. Correct Answer: B
64 rounds down to 60: 8 x 60 = 480.
Incorrect Answers:
A. 64 was incorrectly rounded up to 70: 8 x 70 = 560.
C. 64 was incorrectly rounded up to 70, and then a multiplication error occurred.
D. This is the exact answer; it is not an estimate.

51. Correct Answer: A
Round the total number of pencils per box (64) to the nearest ten (60). 60 pencils per box x 9 boxes = 540 pencils.
Incorrect Answers:
B. The number of pencils per box was incorrectly rounded up to 70: 70 pencils per box x 9 boxes = 630 pencils.
C. The number of pencils per box was rounded up to the nearest five: 65 pencils per box x 9 boxes = 585 pencils.
D. 576 is the exact answer; it is not an estimate.

52. Correct Answer: B
61 rounds down to 60: 60 x 6 = 360.
Incorrect Answers:
A. 59 rounds up to 60: 60 x 5 = 300.
C. 55 rounds up to 60: 60 x 5 = 300.
D. 69 rounds up to 70: 70 x 6 = 420.

Explanations for Test C Answers *(cont.)*

Fractions *(page 73)*

53. Correct Answer: B
The total number of segments between 0 and 1 is 9, which is the denominator. The number of segments between 0 and the dot is 5, which is the numerator. The fraction shown on the number line is $\frac{5}{9}$.

Incorrect Answers:

A. The total number of segments between 0 and 1 would be 10, and the number of segments between 0 and the dot would be 5.

C. The total number of segments between 0 and 1 would be 5, and the number of segments between 0 and the dot would be 9.

D. The total number of segments between 0 and 1 would be 9, and the number of segments between 0 and the dot would be 4.

54. Correct Answer: C
The total number of equal parts in the rectangle is 8, which is the denominator. The number of parts shaded in the rectangle is 7, which is the numerator. $\frac{7}{8}$ of the rectangle is shaded.

Incorrect Answers:

A. The total number of equal parts in the rectangle would be 8, and the number of shaded parts would be 1.

B. The total number of equal parts in the rectangle would be 7, and the number of shaded parts would be 8; two rectangles would be needed to show this.

D. The total number of equal parts in the rectangle would be 6, and the number of shaded parts would be 5.

55. Correct Answer: D
The total number of pencils Rob placed on the desk (6) represents the denominator. The number of pencils that did not roll off the desk (4) represents the numerator. The fraction of pencils that did not roll off the desk is $\frac{4}{6}$.

Incorrect Answers:

A. $\frac{2}{6}$ is the fraction of pencils that rolled off the desk.

B. $\frac{6}{2}$ is the reciprocal of the fraction of pencils that rolled off the desk.

C. $\frac{6}{4}$ is the reciprocal of the fraction of pencils remaining on the desk.

56. Correct Answer: C
The total number of cartons of ice cream (5) represents the denominator. The number of chocolate ice cream cartons (2) represents the numerator. $\frac{2}{5}$ of the ice cream is chocolate.

Incorrect Answers:

A. $\frac{5}{2}$ is the reciprocal of the fraction of ice cream that is chocolate.

B. $\frac{3}{5}$ is the fraction of ice cream that is not chocolate.

D. $\frac{1}{5}$ is the fraction of ice cream that is strawberry.

Comparing Fractions *(page 74)*

57. Correct Answer: D
$\frac{5}{10}$, $\frac{3}{6}$, and $\frac{4}{8}$ are all equivalent to $\frac{1}{2}$.

Incorrect Answers:

A. $\frac{5}{10}$, $\frac{3}{6}$, and $\frac{4}{8}$ are all equivalent to $\frac{1}{2}$; therefore, $\frac{5}{10}$ is not greater than the other fractions.

B. $\frac{5}{10}$, $\frac{3}{6}$, and $\frac{4}{8}$ are all equivalent to $\frac{1}{2}$; therefore, $\frac{3}{6}$ is not greater than the other fractions.

C. $\frac{5}{10}$, $\frac{3}{6}$, and $\frac{4}{8}$ are all equivalent to $\frac{1}{2}$; therefore, $\frac{4}{8}$ is not greater than the other fractions.

58. Correct Answer: A
All the numerators are the same (2), therefore the denominators are the clues to the correct answer. The fractions with the greatest denominators have the smallest pieces and are therefore worth less.

Incorrect Answers:

B., C., D. Since all the fractions have the same numerator (2), the fractions with the greatest denominators should be listed first. They have the smallest pieces.

59. Correct Answer: C
To simplify (reduce) a fraction, divide the numerator and denominator by the greatest number that goes evenly into both (greatest common factor).

The GCF of 3 and 6 is 3: $\frac{3}{6} = \frac{1}{2}$.

Incorrect Answers:

A. $\frac{2}{3}$ is greater than $\frac{3}{6}$.

B. $\frac{1}{6}$ is less than $\frac{3}{6}$.

D. $\frac{1}{3}$ is less than $\frac{3}{6}$.

60. Correct Answer: D
Since both $\frac{3}{6}$ and $\frac{4}{8}$ would appear at the same place on the number line as $\frac{1}{2}$, they are equivalent to $\frac{1}{2}$.

Incorrect Answers:

A. $\frac{2}{6}$ and $\frac{1}{3}$ are equivalent fractions, but are less than $\frac{1}{2}$.

B. $\frac{5}{10}$ is equal to $\frac{1}{2}$, but $\frac{2}{5}$ is less than $\frac{1}{2}$.

C. $\frac{2}{4}$ is equal to $\frac{1}{2}$, but $\frac{3}{8}$ is less than $\frac{1}{2}$.

More Fractions *(page 75)*

61. Correct Answer: D
There are 7 segments between 0 and 1; 7 is the denominator.

There are 7 segments between 0 and the dot; 7 is the numerator.

$\frac{7}{7}$ appears at the same location on the number line as the whole number 1.

Incorrect Answers:

A. $\frac{3}{4} < 1$

B. $\frac{6}{7} < 1$

C. $\frac{5}{6} < 1$

62. Correct Answer: C
$\frac{10}{10} = 10 \div 10 = 1$

Incorrect Answers:

A. $\frac{4}{7} = 4 \div 7 \neq 1$; $\frac{4}{7} < 1$

B. $\frac{10}{5} = 10 \div 5 = 2$; > 1

D. $\frac{5}{8} = 5 \div 8 \neq 1$; $\frac{5}{8} < 1$

63. Correct Answer: D
Jose finished $\frac{4}{4}$ of his homework.

$\frac{4}{4} = 4 \div 4 = 1$ whole, or *all* of his homework.

Incorrect Answers:

A. Angela finished $\frac{4}{5}$ of her homework. 4 out of 5 parts is less than the whole thing.

B. Crissy finished $\frac{3}{4}$ of her homework. 3 out of 4 parts is less than the whole thing.

C. Mike finished $\frac{1}{2}$ of his homework. 1 out of 2 is less than the whole thing.

Explanations for Test C Answers *(cont.)*

More Fractions *(page 75) (cont.)*

64. Correct Answer: B

$\frac{10}{5} = 10 \div 5 = 2$

Incorrect Answers:

A. $\frac{2}{2} = 2 \div 2 = 1; 1 \neq 2$

C. $\frac{1}{2} = 1 \div 2 = 0.5; 0.5 \neq 2$

D. 2 is not a fraction

Metric Units *(page 76)*

65. Correct Answer: B

5 mL = about 5 drops of liquid. It is representative of the capacity of a spoon.

Incorrect Answers:

A. 500 mL is about 500 drops of liquid; it is too much for a spoon to hold.

C. 1 L is about 1 quart; it is too much for a spoon to hold.

D. 5 L is about 5 quarts; it is too much for a spoon to hold.

66. Correct Answer: C

250 kg is about 500 pounds; it is the best estimate.

Incorrect Answers:

A. 10 kg is about 20 pounds; a lion weighs more.

B. 250 g is $\frac{1}{4}$ of a kilogram; a lion weighs more.

D. 2,000 g is 2 kg; a lion weighs more.

67. Correct Answer: D

1 mL = 1 drop of water.

1,000 mL = 1L, so 3 L = 3,000 drops of water.

Incorrect Answers:

A. 1,000 drops of water = 1,000 mL = 1L

B. 300 drops of water = 300 mL

C. 30,000 drops of water = 30,000 mL = 30 L

68. Correct Answer: C

Grams measure the weight of small items; it is the best unit of measurement for a nickel.

Incorrect Answers:

A. Kilograms is the best unit of measure for larger weights.

B. Liters measure capacity, not weight.

D. Milliliters measure capacity, not weight.

Two-dimensional Shapes *(page 77)*

69. Correct Answer: A

An obtuse triangle has only one obtuse angle.

Incorrect Answers:

B. An obtuse triangle has two acute angles (and one obtuse angle).

C. An obtuse triangle must have one obtuse angle in order to be called obtuse.

D. A scalene triangle can have one obtuse angle, so a scalene triangle can also be called an obtuse triangle.

70. Correct Answer: B

A square has four equal-length sides and four right angles.

Incorrect Answers:

A. A trapezoid does not have four equal sides; it only has two equal sides. A trapezoid does not have four right angles; it has two acute angles and two obtuse angles.

C. A pentagon has five sides and five angles, not four.

D. An equilateral triangle has three equal sides and three angles, not four.

71. Correct Answer: D

Quadrilaterals are any shapes with four sides.

Incorrect Answers:

A. Quadrilaterals can have any type of angles.

B. A square and a rhombus are both quadrilaterals because they have four sides.

C. A quadrilateral can be any size as long as the shape has four sides and angles.

72. Correct Answer: A

This shape is a polygon because it is a two-dimensional closed shape with at least three straight sides.

Incorrect Answers:

B. A circle is not a polygon because it does not have straight sides.

C. This shape is not a polygon because it is not closed.

D. A cube is not a polygon because it is three-dimensional.

Time to the Half Hour and Quarter Hour *(page 78)*

73. Correct Answer: A

Half past 7 is 7:30. The hour hand is halfway between 7 and 8, and the minute hand is on the 6.

Incorrect Answers:

B. This clock shows half past 8 or 8:30. The hour hand is halfway between 8 and 9, instead of between 7 and 8.

C. This clock shows 7:15. The minute hand is on the 3 instead of the 6.

D. This clock shows 6:40.

74. Correct Answer: D

Quarter to 2 and *45 minutes after 1* both mean 1:45.

Incorrect Answers:

A. *45 minutes after 1* is correct, but *quarter to 1* is incorrect because the hour hand is between 1 and 2, not between 12 and 1.

B. *Quarter to 1* is incorrect because the hour hand is between 1 and 2, not between 12 and 1. *15 minutes to 2* is correct because it is another way to say 1:45.

C. *45 minutes after 1* is the same as 1:45. *15 minutes to 1* is incorrect because the hour hand is between 1 and 2, not between 12 and 1. .

75. Correct Answer: B

The clock shows 9:15, so *45 minutes after 3* does not represent the time shown. The hour and minute hands were reversed: The hour hand is on 9, not on 3, and the minute hand is on 3, not on 9.

Incorrect Answers:

A. *15 minutes after 9* is 9:15.

C. *Quarter after 9* is 9:15.

D. *Nine fifteen* is 9:15 written in words instead of numbers.

76. Correct Answer: D

The game started at half past 10, which is 10:30. Cam arrived at the game at quarter after 10, which is 10:15. 10:15 is 15 minutes before the beginning of the game at 10:30.

Incorrect Answers:

A. Cam arrived at 10:15, which is 15 minutes before the start of the game. If Cam was 30 minutes late, he would have arrived at 11:00.

B. The minutes from 10:30 and 10:15 were added to get 45 minutes: 30 + 15 = 45. The minutes should be subtracted to find the difference between his arrival time and game time.

C. 10:15 is 15 minutes earlier than 10:30, so Cam was not late for the game. If Cam was 15 minutes late, he would have arrived at 10:45.

Explanations for Test C Answers *(cont.)*

Time to the Minute *(page 79)*

77. Correct Answer: B
Phillip was right. The hour hand is between 11 and 12 and the minute hand is on the 7, so the time is 11:35.
Incorrect Answers:
- **A.** Phillip was right, but Ronnie was wrong by 10 minutes. *35 minutes to 12* is 11:25, not 11:35.
- **C.** Ronnie was wrong. The minute hand is on the 7, so it is 25 minutes to 12, not 35.
- **D.** Phillip was right, so both boys were not wrong.

78. Correct Answer: A
The time is 2:18. The hour hand is on 2, and the minute hand is 3 minutes past the number 3.
Incorrect Answers:
- **B.** *Eighteen minutes to 2* is the same as 1:42.
- **C.** The hands on the clock were reversed. The hour hand is on 2, not 4, and the minute hand is between 3 and 4, not on the number 2.
- **D.** The minute hand would be just before the 1 instead of 3 minutes past the number 3.

79. Correct Answer: C
Angelina arrived at 10 minutes to 4, which is the same as 3:50. The class started at 3:40, so she arrived 10 minutes after the start of the class.
Incorrect Answers:
- **A.** If *Angelina arrived 10 minutes early*, she would have arrived at 3:30.
- **B.** Angelina arrived at 3:50.
- **D.** 10 minutes to 4 is the same as 3:50. 3:50 does not mean Angelina was 50 minutes late; it is the time she arrived. 3:50 is only 10 minutes later than 3:40.

80. Correct Answer: B
There are sixty minutes in one hour. Two hours is 60 minutes + 60 minutes = 120 minutes. Add 23 to find the total number of minutes that movie lasted:
2 hours and 23 minutes = 60 + 60 + 23 = 143 minutes.
Incorrect Answers:
- **A.** 83 minutes includes only one hour, instead of two hours: 60 + 23 = 83.
- **C.** 120 minutes includes the two hours only; it does not include the additional 23 minutes.
- **D.** 23 minutes does not include the 2 hours in the total amount of time that the movie lasted.

Elapsed Time *(page 80)*

81. Correct Answer: C
Two hours after 11:45 a.m. is 1:45 p.m.
30 minutes after 1:45 is 2:15 p.m.
Incorrect Answers:
- **A.** 2:15 is correct, but a.m. is incorrect.
- **B.** 2:00 p.m. is 2 hours and 15 minutes after 11:45; the football game was 2 hours and 30 minutes long.
- **D.** 1:45 is 2 hours after 11:45. The game was 2 hours and 30 minutes long.

82. Correct Answer: A
10 minutes to friend's house + 15 minutes to park = 25 minutes. 25 minutes before 1:05 is 12:40.
Incorrect Answers:
- **B.** 1:30 is 25 minutes after Kimberly arrived at the park, instead of 25 minutes before she arrived at the park.
- **C.** 12:55 allows only 10 minutes for Kimberly to walk to the park instead of 25 minutes; it does not include the 15 minutes to walk from her friend's house to the park.
- **D.** 12:50 is the time Kimberly left her friend's house to walk to the park; it does not include Kimberly's 10 minute walk from her house to her friend's house.

83. Correct Answer: B
The time shown on the clock is 3:15.
One hour after 3:15 is 4:15; 20 minutes later is 4:35.
Incorrect Answers:
- **A.** 4:30 would be 1 hour and 15 minutes after 3:15. Bobby picked apples for 1 hour and 20 minutes, which is 5 minutes longer.
- **C.** 4:15 is 1 hour after 3:15. Bobby picked apples for 1 hour and 20 minutes.
- **D.** 3:35 is 20 minutes after 3:15. It does not include the additional hour that Bobby picked apples.

84. Correct Answer: D
10:15 to 12:15 is 2 hours. 12:15 to 12:20 is 5 minutes. Jeffrey played volleyball for 2 hours and 5 minutes.
Incorrect Answers:
- **A.** If Jeffrey played volleyball for *2 hours*, he would have stopped at 12:15, not 12:20. *2 hours* does not include the time between 12:15 and 12:20.
- **B.** If Jeffrey played volleyball for *1 hour and 5 minutes*, he would have stopped at 11:20, not 12:20.
- **C.** If Jeffrey played volleyball for *3 hours and 5 minutes*, he would have stopped at 1:20, not 12:20.

Units of Time *(page 81)*

85. Correct Answer: A
There are 7 days in a week.
10 weeks x 7 days per week = 70 days.
Then add 2 days: 70 + 2 = 72 days.
Incorrect Answers:
- **B.** 52 days was calculated by multiplying 10 weeks x 5 days per week and then adding 2. There are not 5 days in a week; there are 7 days in a week.
- **C.** 12 days was calculated by adding 10 weeks + 2 days. 10 weeks must be converted into days before adding the additional 2 days.
- **D.** 70 days is the number of days in 10 weeks. It does not include the 2 additional days.

86. Correct Answer: C
There are 24 hours in a day.
7 days x 24 hours per day = 168 hours.
Then add 1 hour: 168 + 1 = 169 hours.
Incorrect Answers:
- **A.** 8 hours was calculated by adding 7 days + 1 hour. Convert 7 days into hours before adding.
- **B.** 49 hours was calculated by multiplying 7 days x 7 hours per day, but there are 24 hours in a day, not 7.
- **D.** 168 is the number of hours in 7 days; it does not include the additional hour that Daniel was on vacation.

87. Correct Answer: D
There are 60 minutes in an hour.
3 hours x 60 minutes per hour = 180 minutes.
Then add 45 minutes: 180 + 45 = 225 minutes.
Incorrect Answers:
- **A.** 180 minutes is the number of minutes in 3 hours; it does not include the additional 45 minutes that it took Bonnie to paint her bedroom.
- **B.** 165 minutes would be the time it took Bonnie to paint her bedroom if it took her 2 hours and 45 minutes.
- **C.** 105 minutes would be the time it took Bonnie to paint her bedroom if it took her 1 hour and 45 minutes.

Explanations for Test C Answers *(cont.)*

Units of Time *(page 81)* *(cont.)*

88. Correct Answer: B
Frank did not work 50 days without a day off; he worked 46 days. There are 7 days in a week: 6 weeks x 7 days per week = 42 days. Add 4 days: 42 days + 4 days = 46 days.
Incorrect Answers:
- **A.** Frank only worked 46 days, not 50 days.
- **C.** Frank did not work 50 days, but the number of days he worked was not 42. 42 days was calculated by multiplying 6 weeks x 7 days per week. It does not include the additional 4 days that Frank worked.
- **D.** Frank did not work 50 days, and the number of days he worked was not 34. 34 days was calculated by multiplying 6 weeks x 5 days per week and then adding 4 days to the total. However, there are not 5 days in a week, there are 7 days, so 6 weeks should be multiplied by 7 days per week.

Perimeter *(page 82)*

89. Correct Answer: C
A triangle has three sides, and perimeter is the sum of the lengths of all sides. If each side is 9 units long, then the perimeter is 27 units: 9 + 9 + 9 = 27 units.
Incorrect Answers:
- **A.** Each side cannot be 27 units because the perimeter for the entire triangle is 27 units.
- **B.** There are four measurements given, and a triangle only has three sides.
- **D.** The perimeter of this figure would be 26 units.

90. Correct Answer: B
A rectangle with length 6 in. and width 2 in. has a perimeter of 16 in. A rectangle with length 8 in. and width 1 in. has a perimeter of 18 in. 18 in. ≠ 16 in.
Incorrect Answers:
- **A.** A rectangle with length 4 in. and width 4 in. has a perimeter of 16 in.
- **C.** A rectangle with length 7 in. and width 1 in. has a perimeter of 16 in.
- **D.** A rectangle with length 5 in. and width 3 in. has a perimeter of 16 in.

91. Correct Answer: D
Perimeter is calculated by adding all the sides:
3 cm + 2 cm + 7 cm + 2 cm + 4 cm = 19 cm.
Incorrect Answ ers:
- **A.** 17 cm does not include all sides of the figure; a 2-cm side was not included in the total.
- **B.** In. is the wrong label.
- **C.** 18 cm does not include all sides of the figure; a 1-cm side was not included in the total.

92. Correct Answer: D
Add all sides of the trapezoid to find the perimeter:
15 m + 15 m + 11 m + 32 m = 73 m.
Incorrect Answers:
- **A.** 43 m was calculated by adding 11 m + 32 m It is not the sum of all the sides.
- **B.** A trapezoid has 4 sides; 30 m. is the sum of only two sides. It does not include the 11 m. side and the 32 m. side in the total.
- **C.** 58 meters is the sum of 15 m + 11 m + 32 m. There are two sides that are 15 meters, not one.

Area *(page 83)*

93. Correct Answer: B
Figures 2 and 3 each have an area of 15 sq. un.
Incorrect Answers:
- **A.** Area of figure 1 is 12 sq. units and figure 2 is 15 sq. units.
- **C.** Area of figure 1 is 12 sq. units and figure 3 is 15 sq. units.

- **D.** Figures 2 and 3 both have areas of 15 sq. units., so *none* is incorrect.

94. Correct Answer: A
$A = l \times w$: 5 m x 5 m = 25 sq. m
Incorrect Answers:
- **B.** 10 sq. m was calculated by adding the length and width.
- **C.** 5 m is the length of one side of the square.
- **D.** 20 sq. m was calculated by adding all the sides. The sum of all sides of a figure is its perimeter.

95. Correct Answer: B
$A = l \times w$: 13 ft. x 8 ft. = 104 sq. ft.
Incorrect Answers:
- **A.** 64 sq. ft. was calculated by multiplying width x width.
- **C.** 21 sq. ft. was calculated by adding length + width.
- **D.** 42 sq. ft. was calculated by adding together the lengths of all sides of the room; this is the perimeter.

96. Correct Answer: D
Divide the shape into two rectangles and find the area of each: 10 in. x 2 in. = 20 sq. in. and 6 in. x 4 in. = 24 sq. in. Add the two areas together: 20 sq. in. + 24 sq. in. = 44 sq. in.
Incorrect Answers:
- **A.** 36 sq. in. was calculated by adding all the sides; this is the perimeter.
- **B.** 32 sq. in. is the area for one part of the figure; it does not include the entire figure.
- **C.** 100 sq. in. was calculated by multiplying the longest length by the longest length: 10 in. x 10 in. This shape was not divided into two shapes first, and all sides were not considered.

Perimeter and Area *(page 84)*

97. Correct Answer: C
$P = (2 \times l) + (2 \times w)$ The perimeter for the rectangle with length 6 m and width of 7 m is 26 m: (2 x 6) + (2 x 7) = 26 m. Rectangle C has the same perimeter: (2 x 12) + (2 x 1) = 26 m.
Incorrect Answers:
- **A.** $P = (2 \times 42) + (2 \times 1) = 86$ m; 86 m ≠ 26 m
- **B.** $P = (2 \times 21) + (2 \times 2) = 46$ m; 46 m ≠ 26 m
- **D.** $P = (2 \times 14) + (2 \times 3) = 34$ m; 34 m ≠ 26 m

98. Correct Answer: C
$A = l \times w$: A = 9 ft. x 5 ft. = 45 sq. ft. $P = (2 \times l) + (2 \times w)$: P = (2 x 9) + (2 x 5) = 28 ft.
Incorrect Answers:
- **A.** 45 sq. ft. is the correct area. The perimeter is 28 ft., not 28 sq. ft.
- **B.** 14 sq. ft. was calculated by adding length + width. 28 ft. is the correct perimeter.
- **D.** The numerical answers were reversed; the area is 45 and the perimeter is 28.

99. Correct Answer: D
$P = (2 \times l) + (2 \times w)$: P = (2 x 24) + (2 x 1) = 50 in. 50 in. is the greatest perimeter.
Incorrect Answers:
- **A.** $P = (2 \times 6) + (2 \times 4) = 20$ in.; 20 < 50
- **B.** $P = (2 \times 12) + (2 \times 2) = 28$ in.; 28 < 50
- **C.** $P = (2 \times 8) + (2 \times 3) = 22$ in.; 22 < 50

100. Correct Answer: B
$A = l \times w$: A rectangle with length 30 cm and width 6 cm would have an area of 180 sq. cm: 30 cm x 6 cm = 180 sq. cm.
Incorrect Answers:
- **A.** A rectangle with length 9 cm and width 4 cm has an area of 36 sq. cm.
- **C.** A rectangle with length 12 cm and width 3 cm has an area of 36 sq. cm.
- **D.** A rectangle with length 6 cm and width of 6 cm has an area of 36 sq. cm.

Bubble Answer Sheet   Test _____

1. Ⓐ Ⓑ Ⓒ Ⓓ	18. Ⓐ Ⓑ Ⓒ Ⓓ	35. Ⓐ Ⓑ Ⓒ Ⓓ	51. Ⓐ Ⓑ Ⓒ Ⓓ	68. Ⓐ Ⓑ Ⓒ Ⓓ	85. Ⓐ Ⓑ Ⓒ Ⓓ
2. Ⓐ Ⓑ Ⓒ Ⓓ	19. Ⓐ Ⓑ Ⓒ Ⓓ	36. Ⓐ Ⓑ Ⓒ Ⓓ	52. Ⓐ Ⓑ Ⓒ Ⓓ	69. Ⓐ Ⓑ Ⓒ Ⓓ	86. Ⓐ Ⓑ Ⓒ Ⓓ
3. Ⓐ Ⓑ Ⓒ Ⓓ	20. Ⓐ Ⓑ Ⓒ Ⓓ	37. Ⓐ Ⓑ Ⓒ Ⓓ	53. Ⓐ Ⓑ Ⓒ Ⓓ	70. Ⓐ Ⓑ Ⓒ Ⓓ	87. Ⓐ Ⓑ Ⓒ Ⓓ
4. Ⓐ Ⓑ Ⓒ Ⓓ	21. Ⓐ Ⓑ Ⓒ Ⓓ	38. Ⓐ Ⓑ Ⓒ Ⓓ	54. Ⓐ Ⓑ Ⓒ Ⓓ	71. Ⓐ Ⓑ Ⓒ Ⓓ	88. Ⓐ Ⓑ Ⓒ Ⓓ
5. Ⓐ Ⓑ Ⓒ Ⓓ	22. Ⓐ Ⓑ Ⓒ Ⓓ	39. Ⓐ Ⓑ Ⓒ Ⓓ	55. Ⓐ Ⓑ Ⓒ Ⓓ	72. Ⓐ Ⓑ Ⓒ Ⓓ	89. Ⓐ Ⓑ Ⓒ Ⓓ
6. Ⓐ Ⓑ Ⓒ Ⓓ	23. Ⓐ Ⓑ Ⓒ Ⓓ	40. Ⓐ Ⓑ Ⓒ Ⓓ	56. Ⓐ Ⓑ Ⓒ Ⓓ	73. Ⓐ Ⓑ Ⓒ Ⓓ	90. Ⓐ Ⓑ Ⓒ Ⓓ
7. Ⓐ Ⓑ Ⓒ Ⓓ	24. Ⓐ Ⓑ Ⓒ Ⓓ	41. Ⓐ Ⓑ Ⓒ Ⓓ	57. Ⓐ Ⓑ Ⓒ Ⓓ	74. Ⓐ Ⓑ Ⓒ Ⓓ	91. Ⓐ Ⓑ Ⓒ Ⓓ
8. Ⓐ Ⓑ Ⓒ Ⓓ	25. Ⓐ Ⓑ Ⓒ Ⓓ	42. Ⓐ Ⓑ Ⓒ Ⓓ	58. Ⓐ Ⓑ Ⓒ Ⓓ	75. Ⓐ Ⓑ Ⓒ Ⓓ	92. Ⓐ Ⓑ Ⓒ Ⓓ
9. Ⓐ Ⓑ Ⓒ Ⓓ	26. Ⓐ Ⓑ Ⓒ Ⓓ	43. Ⓐ Ⓑ Ⓒ Ⓓ	59. Ⓐ Ⓑ Ⓒ Ⓓ	76. Ⓐ Ⓑ Ⓒ Ⓓ	93. Ⓐ Ⓑ Ⓒ Ⓓ
10. Ⓐ Ⓑ Ⓒ Ⓓ	27. Ⓐ Ⓑ Ⓒ Ⓓ	44. Ⓐ Ⓑ Ⓒ Ⓓ	60. Ⓐ Ⓑ Ⓒ Ⓓ	77. Ⓐ Ⓑ Ⓒ Ⓓ	94. Ⓐ Ⓑ Ⓒ Ⓓ
11. Ⓐ Ⓑ Ⓒ Ⓓ	28. Ⓐ Ⓑ Ⓒ Ⓓ	45. Ⓐ Ⓑ Ⓒ Ⓓ	61. Ⓐ Ⓑ Ⓒ Ⓓ	78. Ⓐ Ⓑ Ⓒ Ⓓ	95. Ⓐ Ⓑ Ⓒ Ⓓ
12. Ⓐ Ⓑ Ⓒ Ⓓ	29. Ⓐ Ⓑ Ⓒ Ⓓ	46. Ⓐ Ⓑ Ⓒ Ⓓ	62. Ⓐ Ⓑ Ⓒ Ⓓ	79. Ⓐ Ⓑ Ⓒ Ⓓ	96. Ⓐ Ⓑ Ⓒ Ⓓ
13. Ⓐ Ⓑ Ⓒ Ⓓ	30. Ⓐ Ⓑ Ⓒ Ⓓ	47. Ⓐ Ⓑ Ⓒ Ⓓ	63. Ⓐ Ⓑ Ⓒ Ⓓ	80. Ⓐ Ⓑ Ⓒ Ⓓ	97. Ⓐ Ⓑ Ⓒ Ⓓ
14. Ⓐ Ⓑ Ⓒ Ⓓ	31. Ⓐ Ⓑ Ⓒ Ⓓ	48. Ⓐ Ⓑ Ⓒ Ⓓ	64. Ⓐ Ⓑ Ⓒ Ⓓ	81. Ⓐ Ⓑ Ⓒ Ⓓ	98. Ⓐ Ⓑ Ⓒ Ⓓ
15. Ⓐ Ⓑ Ⓒ Ⓓ	32. Ⓐ Ⓑ Ⓒ Ⓓ	49. Ⓐ Ⓑ Ⓒ Ⓓ	65. Ⓐ Ⓑ Ⓒ Ⓓ	82. Ⓐ Ⓑ Ⓒ Ⓓ	99 Ⓐ Ⓑ Ⓒ Ⓓ
16. Ⓐ Ⓑ Ⓒ Ⓓ	33. Ⓐ Ⓑ Ⓒ Ⓓ	50. Ⓐ Ⓑ Ⓒ Ⓓ	66. Ⓐ Ⓑ Ⓒ Ⓓ	83. Ⓐ Ⓑ Ⓒ Ⓓ	100. Ⓐ Ⓑ Ⓒ Ⓓ
17. Ⓐ Ⓑ Ⓒ Ⓓ	34. Ⓐ Ⓑ Ⓒ Ⓓ		67. Ⓐ Ⓑ Ⓒ Ⓓ	84. Ⓐ Ⓑ Ⓒ Ⓓ	